taste of beirut

Delicious Lebanese Recipes from
Classics to Contemporary to Mezzes and More

Joumana A

Health Communications, Inc.
Deerfield Beach, Florida

www.hcibooks.com

**Library of Congress Cataloging-in-Publication Data
is available from the Library of Congress**

ISBN-13: 978-0-7573-1770-5 (paperback)
ISBN-10: 0-7573-1770-7 (paperback)
ISBN-13: 978-0-7573-1771-2 (e-book)
ISBN-10: 0-7573-1771-5 (e-book)

Publisher: Health Communications, Inc.
            3201 S.W. 15th Street
            Deerfield Beach, FL 33442–8190

Photography © Joumana Accad
Cover design by Dane Wesolko
Interior design and formatting by Lawna Patterson Oldfield

Contents

Chapter 3: Breads, Breakfast, and Brunch

Chapter 4: Sandwiches and Soups

Sandwiches

Soups

Chapter 5: Mezzes: Dips, Finger Foods, Salads, and Sides

Dips

Finger Foods

Salads and Sides

Chapter 6: Main Courses

Meals in a Jiffy (Thirty Minutes to One Hour)

Stews *(Yakhneh)* and Stuffed Veggies *(Mahashee)*

Rice, Grains, Pasta, and Legumes

Kibbeh

Seafood Dishes

Chapter 7: Desserts

Introduction

Born and raised in Beirut, Lebanon, I learned culinary traditions upon the heels of my grandmother (Teta Nabiha), who was in charge of feeding us. She was a true artist, and I would sit by her side and watch her create masterpieces: gossamer dumplings, thin as muslin; *kibbeh* balls rolled to a one-eighth-inch wall; meat pies that she'd patiently stretch out, dipping her fingers in olive oil; turnovers, evenly pinched and tightly sealed by hand.

She'd do her daily marketing by lowering her straw basket, suspended on a rope and pulley, out the window and down to the market four stories below. From above she would inspect the fresh veggies to make sure they were the proper size and free of soft spots. She'd haggle with the vendors and confer with the butcher and the fishmonger.

The rhythms of life in Lebanon were unhurried, meaningful, and steeped in tradition. Food—both the preparation and the consumption—was a celebration of life, something to be savored and enjoyed. The ingredients were always fresh, the vegetables in season, and meat was eaten only once a week or on special occasions.

In 1979, I moved to the United States, where I spent the next thirty years. While raising my American children, I attempted the quixotic task of combining my Lebanese heritage with my fast-paced life, wistfully wishing I could somehow make the two worlds mesh. With so very little leisure time, Americans wanted their food to be convenient and eaten in a hurry, which often meant dishes that came fully prepared from the freezer aisle or a drive-thru window. While this might serve a need, the food is often bland and not the best nutritionally. I wanted to pass on the traditions of my homeland, to show that it is possible to eat delicious *and* nutritious food—without having to spend hours over a stove.

Since coming to the United States, the American food scene has grown by leaps and bounds. In this book, I will show you how to bring Lebanese tastes and techniques to your home. My philosophy about cooking exemplifies what I believe is a common thread for Lebanese culinary artists: striving to reach the highest flavor quotient with the smallest number of basic ingredients. Lebanese cuisine is not for the sophisticate; it is for the person who values *conviviality* above all else.

Through easy step-by-step instructions, I will teach you that it is possible for someone with limited time to cook Lebanese-inspired meals—many of them in one hour or less. You will discover a cuisine that is rich and varied, sourced on natural and fresh vegetables and foods. *Taste of Beirut* will bring the healthful and fabulous flavors of my homeland to your family table.

Do's and Don'ts of Lebanese Cooking and Eating

1. *Pita bread is served with every meal in Lebanon.* Pita bread is served at every single meal, and comes in three sizes: large (for sandwiches), medium (for dips or as a utensil), and cocktail-size. Pita bread in Lebanon is very thin, less than one-sixteenth inch thin. When ready to serve a meal, use kitchen scissors to cut each piece of bread into four triangles, put them back in the plastic bag, tie and fold the bag, and place it on the table to pass around at the next meal. The unused bread can be stored in the back of the refrigerator without risk of drying out.

   Bread is used as a utensil at the Lebanese table; you can forget forks or spoons—just don't forget the fresh bread! Pita bread freezes well and can be thawed at the last minute. The bread will warm up gently to room temperature while you set the table and prepare salad.

   Leftover pita bread is cut into croutons, fried in oil, and drained; most people nowadays prefer it toasted in the oven at 300 degrees F until golden brown. Fried pita-bread croutons are sprinkled on salads (*fattoush*), as a crunchy layer on all the casseroles (*fatteh*), as a binding ingredient for veggie side dishes (*treedeh*), or fried with grilled fish. Toasted pita croutons will keep for a couple of weeks in a tightly closed container in a cupboard.

2. *Lemons are used daily.* Press fresh lemon juice and keep it in an ice-cube tray in the freezer. Do the same with orange juice or other citrus juice used in cooking *tarator* sauce (the Lebanese equivalent of mayonnaise) or pudding. Whenever needed, an ice cube of lemon juice can be retrieved

3

easily enough. Lemon juice is used daily in just about everything: salad dressing, sprinkled over soups or stews, when making tarator sauces, and in making *mezze* items. If time allows, the lemon rind can be grated (first, then press the juice) and stored in a small bag in the freezer with a tablespoon of olive oil, to throw in a soup or stew at the last minute for a boost of flavor.

3. *Keep onions on hand.* Chop them and sauté them in oil until golden and store in freezer bags with the oil for each dish you are planning to make for the next couple of weeks. Almost every dish requires onions sautéed in olive oil until soft or golden, therefore, having the equivalent of three bags will amply take care of the weekly meals.

4. *Use fresh garlic cloves.* There is a huge difference in flavor (and nutritional benefits) between fresh and old garlic, so I'd recommend local or at least domestic garlic as opposed to imported. Peel a few garlic cloves; if there is a green shoot, remove it and discard it (the garlic is old). Keep the peeled cloves in a closed jar in the fridge to use when needed.

   I also like to keep a **garlic mortar** handy to make **garlic paste,** which can go into salad dressing, stews, soups, yogurt cheese dips, side dishes, or anything you have cooking on your stove.

5. *Fresh herbs are best.* Cilantro and parsley are "blessed" in the Lebanese mindset. Cilantro gives flavor to veggies, stews, and soups. Parsley is the main component of tabbouleh salad and is sprinkled on just about everything else. When possible, use Lebanese parsley, which is delicate, flat-leaved, and silky. So-called Italian parsley is too thick, so I'd recommend organic Italian parsley as a substitute. Wash, dry one or two bunches of each, and keep in a sealed container covered with a kitchen towel.

   Toss in cilantro pesto at the last minute to add flavor or use it to liven up chicken wings, shrimp, fish, or other chicken dishes. Try it on cubed potatoes, carrots, or taro (or any veggie for that matter). Use it for soups, stews, bean stews, lentils, and in *mulukhieh.* To save time, make a dozen portions of cilantro pesto and freeze them in an ice-cube tray or in small freezer bags.

6. *Keep extra-virgin olive oil in a cruet, always on the table.* I'd recommend one imported from Lebanon with a Fair Trade emblem on the bottle. Lebanese farmers drink a sip of the olive oil to make sure it is

fit for consumption. If the taste is bitter or too peppery, it is probably bad. Believed to give you superhuman strength and immunity, olive oil is added to yogurt cheese (*labneh*) in the morning, salad or baked potato, soup or stews, on *zaatar* spice mix—in short, at every meal every single day of a Lebanese person's life. Olive oil has a mythical aura in the Lebanese folk mindset, as a proverb says, "Drink your olive oil and break through the wall" (*kol zeit w-entah el-heyt*).

7. *Simplify your spice rack.* Traditional Lebanese cooking uses these main spices easily found in your grocery store: cinnamon, allspice (Jamaican pepper), black pepper, white pepper, and nutmeg. There is no need to stock your pantry with a plethora of spices unless you are planning a specific pastry or dish. In Lebanese cuisine, cinnamon is used for savory cooking, and rarely for sweet baking.

8. *Incorporate olives into every meal.* Olives are called the "sheikh of the table" (*sheikh el-sofrah*) for a reason, as they are served for breakfast, lunch, and dinner. At breakfast, olives are served with yogurt cheese, sliced tomatoes, cucumbers, and fresh mint leaves. At lunch, the meal will start with one nestled in a tiny piece of pita bread, just to open the appetite. At dinner, they accompany a sliver of hard cheese, like a *kashkaval* or *halloumi*, with a side of green beans in tomato stew (*loobyeh bel-zeit*), for a light and frugal dinner. As the saying goes, "Bread and olives is the best life can offer" (*khobz wzeitoon, ahsan maykoon*). Lebanese folks have always believed that frugal living off the earth's bounty, in this case, the olive trees and the wheat fields (bulgur), are sufficient for one's good health and happiness.

9. *Tahini* is another very important flavoring in the Lebanese kitchen. Consumed daily, tahini provides 20 percent of the calcium requirement in the Lebanese diet. I'd highly recommend a good Lebanese brand, and that you keep one in the cupboard at all times. Tahini is the main component of tarator sauce, *hummus* (in all its variations), and tuna *tagen* or *kibbeh*. Tarator is made in a jiffy with lemon juice and garlic paste, and can dress any cooked seasonal veggie with a pleasant result (potato, green beans, chard, beets, cauliflower, and eggplant).

10. *Yogurt and labneh.* Yogurt is essential in a Lebanese kitchen. Labneh, which is yogurt cheese, can be made overnight by simply draining the

yogurt and adding salt. Yogurt is uncooked for salad or served as a side dish with bulgur pilafs or kebabs, or as a simple meal with plain rice to help cure a tummy ache. Yogurt is cooked as a soup or a stew. It is one of the layers in many casseroles, or is made into a sauce with meat chunks or kibbeh balls. It can be made with either cow's or goat's milk. Goat yogurt is considered finer, more stable to cook with, and much healthier. Ideally, a small dairy farm would supply the yogurt, which could be perpetually remade at home. Making yogurt is easy and does not require a special tool, machine, or skill.

11. *Legumes.* Legumes (chickpeas, white beans, yellow fava beans, lentils) can be bought canned, rinsed, and reheated in fresh water, or bought dried, soaked overnight, cooked until soft, and stored in freezer bags with one cup of cooking water in one-meal servings. Grab a bag from the freezer when needed and make hummus on the spur of the moment or add to a stew.

12. *Meats and poultry.* Cook ground meat ahead of time with onions and spices. Earmark each bag for one meal. Freeze and grab it later when needed to stuff kibbeh or veggies, or for rice and spiced meat.

13. *Lamb confit.* If you are cooking with lamb, store all the residual lamb fat and lamb bits in the freezer in small bags, tightly sealed. Use it to fry eggs sunny-side-up *(beyd bel-awarma)* in the morning. Simply melt the lamb fat in a skillet over medium heat, slide the eggs into the pan, and fry until the whites are set. Season to taste and serve with pita bread. Another use for lamb fat: Add it to the kibbeh stuffing instead of meat; this is the method used in the rural areas to make do when meat is scarce. A tiny bit of lamb fat can replace lamb confit. Lamb confit was made every fall to stock up the larder. It was kept in jars to use throughout the year to flavor stews, soups, kibbeh, or fried eggs. This is an easy and practical alternative.

14. *Nuts are essential.* Stock up on pine nuts, almonds, pistachios, walnuts, and sesame seeds. Store them in the fridge or freezer. Boil the almonds or pistachios in separate pans for a couple of minutes, drain on paper towels, and peel when they have cooled, then airdry and store. Sesame seeds can be dry-roasted in a skillet over gentle heat for about thirty minutes until golden, then cooled and stored. All nuts should be kept in small freezer bags. When nuts are used in a recipe, always fry the peeled nuts in a bit of butter or oil until caramel-colored.

CHAPTER 1

The Lebanese Larder

Lebanon has recently garnered a flattering
reputation for its cuisine from all corners of the globe;
it is remarkable that such a small country
(with a population of around 4 million people)
brings so much attention worldwide to its food.
The good news is that most Lebanese cooking uses
simple, everyday ingredients found in any market.
The spice rack in a traditional Lebanese kitchen is also
very modest and consists of basic, well-known spices.
This section sheds some light on the few specific
Lebanese staples, such as bulgur, and the more exotic
items such as mastic or sumac. These are easily
found in all ethnic or Mediterranean markets
or through online food purveyors.

BREAD, GRAINS, PASTA, AND RICE

Breads

The overwhelming majority of bread produced in Lebanon in small or medium-size commercial ovens is the pita bread known in the West. It differs from Western pita bread in that it is much larger and thinner (12–14 inches wide and very thin). It comes in white or dark flour. The other size available is about 9 inches wide. There is also a cocktail size available, perfect for *mezzes* (cocktail parties), in which the tiny breads get stuffed and displayed on large trays.

Pita bread always needs to be kept in a plastic bag to prevent drying; however, it freezes very well. Buying several bags and keeping them stored in the freezer is a good idea. They will easily defrost at room temperature.

Bulgur (Burghul)

There are two main types of bulgur: fine bulgur, used to make kibbeh or tabbouleh salad, and coarse bulgur, used to make pilafs. These types of bulgur are sold numbered, with the fine variety bearing numbers ranging from #1 to #2 and the coarse #3 to #4. In addition, bulgur can be dark-colored or yellow-colored. In Lebanon, some cooks like to pick different colors for different kibbeh, choosing yellow for pumpkin or fish kibbeh and dark for meat kibbeh. It is simply a matter of personal preference; I have seen both colors on display at Middle Eastern stores in the United States.

Cracked Wheat (Jreesh)

This is a fine cracked wheat. The difference between jreesh and bulgur #1 (both look similar) is that jreesh is not parboiled as bulgur but rather ground up into tiny pellets the size of fine bulgur (#1) or a bit coarser. Jreesh is popular in the south and is mixed with the dough of a bread called *mishtah*. Some bakeries in Beirut will make breakfast flatbreads (*man'ooshe*) with jreesh, advertising this fact on their menus. The flatbread made with jreesh looks speckled with brown dots and has a deeper, more rustic flavor than the flatbreads made with white flour only. Jreesh is also used in lieu of regular fine bulgur when making some types of kibbeh in some communities and in other Arab countries like Iraq.

Lebanese Couscous (Moghrabieh)

This is the Lebanese equivalent of couscous, and it is made with semolina. In Lebanon, *moghrabieh* comes from Maghreb, a word used to designate all countries in North Africa (as opposed to Mashriq, all countries in the Middle East). Some specialty shops in Lebanon provide it fresh;

cooking it fresh involves steaming the grains by using a similar technique as the North African couscous. However, all exported moghrabieh is dry and needs to be parboiled for about five minutes in water, then cooked gradually in a flavorful broth, one ladle of broth at a time. It is sold dry in packages in the United States. In Lebanon, moghrabieh is also the name of a hearty casserole made with the actual moghrabieh grain and chicken (or meat). In some communities, couscous is made with wheat, bulgur, and water, and is called *maftoul*. This grain remains a regional one (handmade in some Syrian and Palestinian communities); however, I have found it imported in the United States at upscale kitchen stores. It cooks easily, just like rice, and has a distinct earthy taste; because it is handmade, the grains are uneven in size.

Short- and Long-Grain Rice

The two main types of rice used in the Lebanese kitchen are starchy short-grain and long-grain rice (such as American long-grain or Indian basmati). The starchy short-grain rice is preferred for stuffing veggies or making rice puddings, as the longer cooking time softens the grains considerably until they meld into the sauce. The long-grain rice is better suited for pilafs, such as the ground meat and spice pilaf served with turkey or chicken for holiday celebrations. The short-grain rice is imported from Italy, Egypt, or Turkey; the long-grain rice is the American long-grain rice or basmati.

Roasted Green Wheat (Freekeh)

Another grain worth exploring is roasted green wheat, or freekeh. Freekeh is an ancient grain that is experiencing a resurgence in popularity due to its extraordinary nutritional benefits and wonderful smoky taste.

Freekeh is wheat that is picked while it is still green and then smoked. It exudes a wonderful aroma while it is cooking over the stove. It also has more minerals than all the other grains and is highly recommended for weight loss. Freekeh is sold in Middle Eastern stores and online, in bulk or in boxes. It needs to be rinsed carefully prior to cooking. Freekeh is offered in two main varieties: whole-grain and broken grain. If the whole-grain type is used, the cooking time must be increased by at least one-third and the amount of liquid increased as well.

Semolina (Smeed and Ferkha)

There are two main types of semolina that are used in the Lebanese kitchen: a coarse semolina and a fine semolina. If using the coarse semolina to make pastry, the pastry will be crumbly. Conversely, if using the fine one, it will hold together better, like regular flour. Coarse semolina is called *smeed* and fine semolina is called *ferkha*.

Semolina is a type of flour made from durum wheat. Durum wheat is a strong variety of wheat that has been cultivated in Lebanon for thousands of years ("durum" means "strong" in Latin). In fact, the Bekaa Valley in the country used to supply the Roman Empire with wheat, grapes, and other foods. The durum wheat used to make semolina is high in protein and low in gluten. Both grades of semolina are sold in all Middle Eastern markets, and in Latino, Greek, Turkish, Persian, or health-food stores in North America. If you are unable to find semolina, a good substitute is to use the American Cream of Wheat cereal (farina).

In Lebanon, semolina is sold everywhere and is used to make cakes (*nammura, ma'amoul, kaak*) and pastries, to thicken puddings (*mamounieh, layali lubnan, basbusa, khabeesah, tamrieh, kellage*), or as an ingredient in bread-making. Semolina flour is also used to make pasta.

Vermicelli (Sh'areeyeh)

Pasta in the Lebanese diet consists of vermicelli, always combined with rice for the traditional pilaf served with stews. The vermicelli is bought dry, fried in butter, and cooked with rice. Homemade pasta, *sheesh barak* (a type of tiny ravioli), is the other main pasta dish. Nowadays, most people buy this pasta frozen in the supermarkets to save time. It is not exported and may be replaced with an Italian filled pasta, such as tortellini. Finally, there is a type of pasta called *ma'karoon,* similar to the Italian gnocchi, that is prepared mainly in rural areas.

Wheat Berries

The wheat berries used in Lebanese cooking are dried wheat berries, which are available whole or shelled for a lighter or bleached version. The unpeeled wheat berries take about one hour to cook (or longer) and need to be soaked overnight. The shelled variety berry is also available in markets. It can be rinsed, placed in a pot with about six cups of water, and brought to a boil. The wheat berry can be boiled the day before and soaked in water covered with a towel. The next day, it is simmered for a while longer, until it is thoroughly cooked. This process reduces the cooking time somewhat. Conversely, the berries can simply be simmered in liquid for one hour or longer, until the grains are cooked.

PASTES, PASTRIES, SEASONINGS, SPICE MIXES, AND SWEETENERS

Carob Molasses *(Dibs el Kharroub)*

This is a thick syrup made by soaking milled carob pods in water and reducing the extracted liquid. The carob tree has a history of use dating back to ancient times. It is also known as Saint John's bread, for it is said that John the Baptist survived in the desert by eating carob. In Lebanon, carob molasses was traditionally used as an alternative to sugar. Mixed with tahini, it is still eaten as a dessert called *dibs be theeneh* (see "Desserts" Chapter 7, under "Carob Molasses and Tahini").

Pomegranate Molasses *(Dibs al-Rumman)*

Pomegranates thrive in Lebanon and this comes in handy in the mountains where citrus is difficult to grow (citrus grows mainly in the coastal areas). There are two main varieties of pomegranate trees: sour and sweet. The sour ones are used for molasses. The sweet pomegranates are just savored as a fruit or as a topping for pudding. The fruity and tangy flavor of pomegranate molasses is used in savory dishes, such as kebabs, turnovers, meat pies, stews, or kibbeh stuffing. A touch of pomegranate molasses is sometimes added to dips, such as the eggplant dip baba ghanouj or red pepper dip (muhammara). It can be diluted with water and mixed with olive oil to make a salad dressing. Pomegranate molasses should not be substituted for other types of molasses, such as carob or grape.

Grape Molasses (*Dibs el Enab*)

A friend of my mother's, Milady, who lives by herself in her family's home in the mountains in Lebanon, invited me over one day. She offered me some of her homemade grape molasses for breakfast with some pita bread. It tasted just like toffee! You can purchase this heavenly sweet food at Arab and specialty shops in North America, as it is a food also made in Turkey, Greece, and Cyprus. The best grape molasses is a golden color and is called "whipped" (*madroub*). Many desserts (puddings) and cookies are still made using grape molasses instead of sugar in rural areas.

Halvah (*Halawa*)

Halvah is called *halawa* in Lebanon and is one of the most popular candies or confections. It is sold in every remote neighborhood market, either plain or with pistachios or chocolate swirled into it. It is a mixture of tahini and syrup. In Lebanon, most kids at one time or another (especially in past generations) had halawa roll-ups to tide over their hunger while in school. Even now, I am told, halawa is a breakfast of choice among inmates.

There are many manufacturers of halvah in Lebanon, with some main ones established in certain cities. Halvah is a very versatile food; it can be incorporated into custards, ice creams, cookie dough, breads, or even beverages. Its distinct sweet tahini taste is one that elicits instant love or rejection.

Kataifi, Kadaifi, or Osmalliyeh

This pastry is sold in North America under the name *kataifi* or *kadaifi*. In Lebanon, it is called *osmalliyeh* and is available fresh at specialty shops or frozen at supermarkets. This is the pastry that is used to make hundreds of Arabic pastries. It is available at some specialty supermarkets, at all Greek and Middle Eastern groceries, and online. It comes frozen in one-pound packages or dried in coils (not frozen), imported from Turkey. Lately, it has been made available in mainstream supermarkets as well. If you buy it frozen, it needs to thaw overnight in the fridge before using.

Lamb Confit (Awarma)

Every Lebanese older than eighty who lived in a mountain village remembers making *awarma* for sustenance throughout the year. Awarma is lamb cooked in its own fat. Historically, the lamb was slaughtered on a special occasion, and after the main meat sections were distributed to the community, awarma was made with the leftover bits. Fat was taken from the lamb tail and the bits of lamb were added to the fat and cooked, then preserved in a jar for several months. One tablespoon of awarma was sufficient to flavor any food, be it a stew, stuffing for kibbeh, or turnovers.

It is still an economical way to add meat flavor to a dish. As lamb tail fat is not sold in North America, one option is to collect all the lamb fat from different cuts and store it in the freezer. When needed, remove a small quantity, fry it with onions (or ground meat), and add it to a soup or stew. This recipe is from Rabih, a young butcher in Beirut: Melt one pound of lamb fat over very low heat in a deep pot. Sprinkle one pound of lean ground lamb with one teaspoon allspice and add it to the pot. Let the lamb cook in its own fat for forty-five minutes over very low heat, adding one teaspoon of salt to it halfway through, stirring it constantly and watching so that the meat does not burn. Transfer the mixture to a sterilized jar and store in the refrigerator for six months.

Mahlab Cherry Spice (Mahlab)

Mahlab is a spice used frequently in Lebanese baking. Nearly all specialty breads add it for that elusive flavor (a mix between bitter almond and nutmeg). It is available in all ethnic stores, as it is also used by the Greeks, Turks, and Persians, among others, and is available in two forms: kernels (beige-colored seeds) or powder.

Mahlab is actually extracted from the pits of a certain variety of black cherries (*Prunus mahaleb*, also known as the Saint Lucie cherry). I prefer to get the kernels and grind them in a coffee grinder when needed, as the powder tends to go rancid fairly quickly (within a year), developing an unbearable putrid smell.

Mastic (Meskeh)

Mastic or *meskeh* is a flavoring used in Lebanese cuisine in both savory and sweet dishes. It is added to the beef *shawarma* marinade (shawarma refers to the process where meats are put on a spit and slow-grilled), or certain pilafs or stews. It is used with ice cream, jams, puddings, or holy bread. Mastic is fragrant, like musk. In the past it was used as a medicine, a breath freshener (in the sultan's harem), and for reducing oral bacteria or gingivitis when chewed; it contains antioxidants.

Mastic is currently collected from the native trees that secrete it (it is a natural resin) in the island of Chios in Greece, and then dried and sold. In Lebanese grocery stores, mastic is always strategically placed by the cash register, bagged in tiny cellophane packages glued on a cardboard placard bearing the sign: True Greek brand (*Yunaneh asleh*). In North America, look for it in Arab, Greek, or Turkish stores or online (*mastiha* in Greek).

To use mastic, a small mortar and pestle is needed (preferably made with marble or stone). Grind a few pebbles (a tiny bit goes a long way) of mastic with a teaspoon of salt for a savory dish, or sugar for a sweet dish, until powdery (or it will never dissolve in the food!). You can also grind it using a rolling pin in between sheets of wax paper. Always keep your mastic in the fridge in a closed jar or bag.

Orange Blossom Water and Rose Water

The two main flavorings in Lebanese desserts, pastries, jams, confections, and sweet breads are rose water and orange blossom water. Rose

water is the distilled water of rose petals of a certain type of rose, *Rosa damascena* (*al-ward al-joory*). Orange blossom water is distilled from the blossoms of a variety of oranges called Seville oranges (*busfeyr*). In addition to providing an exquisite and delicate flavor to sweets, these two waters have also been used to soothe mild burns or certain skin conditions. Both this rose variety and the Seville orange are cultivated in the United States. Artisan waters can be found in some markets or online.

Orchid Powder *(Sahlab)*

Sahlab is a white powder extracted from a variety of wild orchids found in large quantities in Turkey. Sahlab is not sold in North America. What is available instead is a sahlab mix that does not contain any real sahlab; instead, the sahlab mix uses starch, sugar, and flavoring. I have only found real sahlab in Turkey in the bazaars in Istanbul and Beirut, as well as other cities in the region. It is a rare ingredient. When added to ice cream, sahlab makes it famously chewy. It thickens puddings and drinks, and has an exotic flavor.

Phyllo Dough *(Rkakat, Kellage, Baklawa)*

This paper-thin pastry is available in every single Middle Eastern market and even in many main supermarkets. The only difficulty in handling it is the fact that it dries up rapidly and needs to be covered at all times while being handled. It is the dough that has been used for centuries for baklava and similar pastries from the edges of the Ottoman Empire all the way to the Persian Empire.

Southern Lebanese Spice Mix *(Kammuneh)*

A Southern Lebanese spice mix, *kammuneh* is added to bulgur, which turns it bright green. It is also blended with raw meat for *frakeh*, the Southern Lebanese style of kibbeh tartare. Kammuneh can also be combined with potatoes for a vegetarian potato kibbeh, or tomatoes for a tomato kibbeh plate. It is used in Southern Lebanese cuisine and is made of dried and fresh spices. Salam, a charming lady I met at the beauty salon, who told me she was from the south, brought me a sample one morning gathered by her mother. She said, "Just go out in the fields and gather anything you see or smell that is fragrant." In her little pouch, her *kammuneh* had rose petals, wild marjoram, wild mint, basil, and sage; to complete the spice mixture, cumin powder, anise powder, dried mint, and red chili powder was added. There are no set rules as long as the mixture is heady and fragrant, and most of the herbs are wild. The addition of rose petals to a spice mix for meat (kibbeh) may seem strange, but it gives out the most tantalizing taste.

Sumac

Sumac is a wild bush that grows all over the Lebanese mountains; it can get quite tall (over six feet) and looks from a distance like clusters of red grapes with small seeds. Because citrus does not grow at the higher altitudes, it is an ideal way for mountain villagers (mountains constitute more than half of the Lebanese topography) to add a delightful sour and lemony taste to food. Along with great flavor, sumac is chock-full of health benefits as well. When buying sumac at a store, beware of the sumac that is bright red, as it is most likely dyed. Smell it immediately; it should have a lemony scent. If unable to source good sumac, replace it with lemon or a pinch of citric acid (sold in Middle Eastern stores in a white powder spice bag). Sumac is not only used to flavor fattoush salad

dressing but is also one of the main components of zaatar mix. Sumac is also added to dozens of stews or kibbeh stuffings.

Tahini

Tahini is a paste obtained by crushing hulled white sesame seeds between two large stones. The word "tahini" is taken from the Arabic root verb meaning "to grind."

There are various grades of tahini; the best are considered to be the lighter-colored or beige varieties. Tahini is a natural product and does not contain any additives or preservatives. It is considered by many to be a health food due to the abundance of its nutrients. A serving of tahini has eighty-nine calories and contains both carbohydrates and protein, and the fat in tahini is mostly healthy, with a high concentration of omega-3 and omega-6 fatty acids. Tahini boasts a large amount of beneficial minerals, such as copper and phosphorus, and vitamins, such as thiamine. Once opened, a jar of tahini has a shelf life of about six months. As the oil in the tahini tends to separate, a solution for this is to keep the jar upside down or stir the oil back into the paste prior to use.

Tahini has a subtle, nutty taste and is used in Middle Eastern countries the way mayonnaise or butter is traditionally used in the Western world. There are hundreds of dishes containing tahini, and it is present at almost every meal.

CHAPTER 2

Basics in the Lebanese Kitchen

Lebanese cuisine has won raves the world over, yet it is not a complex or sophisticated cuisine; it does, however, require many simple steps. In my mother's time, help was always available in the kitchen to mash some garlic, chop fresh parsley or cilantro, or core and stuff vegetables. Most of us these days do not have the luxury of time or a helper available at one's call. This chapter is intended to make life easier for the home cook by offering time-saving tips and focusing on the simple techniques you can apply over and over on dozens of dishes. Once you practice and gain confidence in a technique such as cooking yogurt, you can apply it to all of the dishes cooked with a yogurt sauce. The same goes for tarator sauce, which is the main component of hummus or baba ghanouj, the dressing in falafel and shawarma, as well as cooked with kibbeh balls or *kafta* paste (a type of meat loaf).

Basic Bulgur Pilaf

YIELD: 4 SERVINGS

(Fine, #1 or #2)

Directions:

Heat the oil in a saucepan over medium heat for 3 minutes. Add the bulgur and stir for a couple of minutes until the grains are well coated with oil. Add the water or stock, sprinkle with salt, and cover. Let the bulgur swell for 5 minutes or so. Serve immediately.

Ingredients:

3 tablespoons olive oil

2 cups bulgur
(*fine, #1 or #2*)

2 cups very hot water or stock *(near simmering)*

Salt, to taste

(Coarse, #3 or #4)

Directions:

1) Transfer the bulgur to a large bowl and soak it in water for 5 minutes; rinse it well.

2) Heat the oil in a saucepan over medium heat for 3 minutes. Add the bulgur and stir for a couple of minutes until the grains are well coated with oil. Add the water or stock, sprinkle with salt, lower the heat, and cover. Let the bulgur simmer gently for 15 minutes or so. Uncover the pan and check to see if it needs more water; if it does, add ¼ cup of water and cook it a few minutes longer until it is soft and chewy. Serve immediately.

Ingredients:

1 cup bulgur
(*coarse, #3 or #4*)

3 tablespoons olive oil

1 cup very hot water or stock *(near simmering)*

Salt, to taste

Cilantro Pesto
(Aliyyet al-Kuzbara)

YIELD: ¼ CUP
This amount is sufficient for a single dish, and if you
want to store extra, just multiply the quantities.

The Italians have their pesto, the French their *pistou*, and the Lebanese have the cilantro pesto commonly called *aliyyet al-kuzbara*. It is a simple mixture of fresh garlic, cilantro, and olive oil, sautéed for mere seconds until the fragrance is released and the ingredients bond together into a paste. This pesto is used to add flavor to stews, potatoes, soups, chicken, fish, and any yogurt sauce, cooked or uncooked. (The same technique is used for coriander pesto, with dry coriander powder.)

The idea is to swirl the mixture into your dish as a final step. This is the secret step that gives the dish an intoxicating kick of flavor. If you like more garlic flavor, by all means bulk up the amount of mashed garlic in this condiment. It is a matter of taste. In addition, the pesto can be conveniently frozen for up to three months in small containers or plastic pouches and pulled out of the freezer at a moment's notice. As a child growing up in Beirut, I knew when the fragrance of frying cilantro was in the air that we would be eating soon—pleasant memories.

Ingredients:

¼ cup olive oil

1 bunch cilantro leaves, washed, dried, and chopped fine, and stems discarded

8 cloves garlic, peeled, chopped, and mashed with 1 teaspoon of salt in a mortar until pasty

NOTE: *If the cilantro bunch is scant, use two instead of one per batch. The amount of chopped cilantro leaves should be at least one ounce or one measuring cup, packed.*

Directions:

Heat the oil in a skillet over medium heat for 3 minutes. Add the cilantro and garlic. The mixture will sizzle, and within seconds a strong fragrance will erupt. Quickly stir the mixture with a wooden spoon to form a paste and then transfer it to a dish or set aside. If not using right away, cool the pesto and transfer to a small freezer bag, date, and store.

NOTE: *I strongly recommend multiplying the recipe to save time. Use ¾ cup olive oil, four bunches of cilantro, and two heads of garlic to maximize your time in the kitchen. Divide the remaining mixture into single servings and freeze. Be sure to freeze uniform amounts that are commonly called for in recipes. For instance, if you frequently use a recipe that calls for ¼ cup pesto, freeze ¼ cup amounts. I have used plastic ice-cube trays for this purpose. You can freeze it in the tray, then pop the frozen cubes into a freezer bag. It's easy to remove a cube (or however many you need) for a recipe. You can also freeze the amount you need in small food-safe plastic bags.*

Citrus-Tahini Sauce *(Arnabiyeh)*

YIELD: 6 CUPS

The sky's the limit here. This citrus-tahini sauce can be customized according to one's taste or what is available fresh, or even what was stored previously in the freezer (which is what most food purveyors resort to in Lebanon). For example, you could use oranges, Seville oranges, blood oranges, grapefruits, clementines, tangerines, tangelos, or lemons.

Directions:

1) Heat the oil in a large saucepan over medium heat. Add the onion slices, cover the pan, and lower the heat. Let the slices soften and stew gently for 15 minutes or so.

2) Pour the tahini into a large pot. Gradually add the citrus juices and water (or stock), stirring until smooth and creamy; pour over the onion slices and stir. Cook gently for 20 minutes. (Add some cornstarch if the sauce is too watery. See note below.)

3) Add the salt and pepper, and pomegranate molasses, if using.

4) Remove from the heat and serve right away or store for a couple of days in the refrigerator.

Ingredients:

⅓ cup oil

3 large onions, sliced

1½ cups tahini *(more if sauce is too watery)*

½ cup orange juice

½ cup Seville, or sour, orange juice

½ cup grapefruit juice

½ cup clementine juice

½ cup tangerine juice

½ cup lemon juice

1 cup water or stock *(depending on the dish)*

1½ teaspoons salt *(or to taste)*

½ teaspoon white pepper

1 teaspoon pomegranate molasses *(optional)*

NOTE: *This sauce is served with taro root, or any boiled vegetable of your choice; it is also served with kibbeh balls for kibbeh arnabiyeh (see Kibbeh Balls in Citrus-Tahini Sauce in Chapter 6 under "Kibbeh"). You can also serve it with boiled chicken or fish. The amount can be halved or doubled and the citrus juices substituted with other fruits, depending on what is available. The taste should be sweet and sour, and the texture creamy. Add the water and juices gradually to the tahini, tasting and only adding more if the sauce is too thick or still curdled. The water is replaced by meat stock when making the kibbeh arnabiyeh; it is used to make the juice taste less acidic and to make the sauce smooth. It should always be added gradually, using more or less as needed. Cornstarch can be mixed with some cold water or juice first, then stirred into the steaming sauce. One tablespoon of cornstarch dissolved in ¼ cup of cold liquid should be sufficient to thicken one cup of sauce. Increase the amount of starch as needed.*

Clarified Butter *(Samneh)*

YIELD: ¾ CUP

Ingredients:

2 sticks unsalted butter
   (8 ounces), cut into cubes

Directions:

Method No. 1:

Place the butter in a saucepan over low heat, letting it melt slowly. Put a large coffee filter or paper towel inside a sieve and place over a heatproof bowl or jar. Once the butter is fully melted, pour it into the sieve. The clarified butter will gradually filter down into the bowl or jar, while the white milk solids will stay caught on the filter. Either discard the milk solids or store them to use later for making cookies (they taste delicious when toasted in a skillet until caramel-colored and incorporated into a cookie dough or tart dough). When the butter is cold, cover the bowl and store in the refrigerator. Clarified butter will keep for 3 months in the refrigerator and can be frozen.

Method No. 2:

Transfer the melted butter to a heatproof glass bowl and place in the refrigerator; the butter will solidify and the milk solids will decant to the bottom after about one hour. Scrape the butter out of the bowl into another bowl and discard the milk solids at the bottom (or keep them to make cheese or other foods).

Dough for Flatbreads, Turnovers, Rolls, and Cocktail-Size Pies

YIELD: 1 BATCH

Directions:

1) Pour ½ cup of the water into a small bowl and sprinkle the yeast and sugar on top. Stir to dissolve and place the bowl in a cupboard or warm place for 5 minutes or so until the mixture bubbles up (this process is called "proofing").

2) Meanwhile, combine the flour and salt in a stand mixer on low speed. With the mixer still running, slowly pour in the oil. Then add the proofed yeast and water mixture and the remaining water.

Ingredients:

1 cup warm water
 (*more as needed*)

2 teaspoons active
 dry yeast

1 teaspoon sugar

3 cups unbleached
 all-purpose flour

1 teaspoon salt

2 tablespoons oil

3) Keep kneading at medium speed for 10 minutes until the dough is smooth, shiny, and pulls away from the sides of the bowl. If the dough is too dry, add a bit more water; if too moist, add in more flour, ½ cup at a time. The amount of water and flour you use depends on the type of flour you've chosen and how high the humidity is on the day you're making it. This is a foolproof recipe, and eventually the dough will take on the right texture—smooth, firm, and supple.

4) Once the dough is the correct consistency, remove it from the mixer and place it into a greased bowl; turn it so that all sides of the dough are coated with oil. Let the dough rise for a couple of hours covered with a damp towel inside a warm place away from drafts, such as a cupboard or an oven. Once you're ready to use it, punch it down and follow your recipe.

NOTE: *If you are not using the dough right away, divide it into two freezer bags and store it in the freezer for a couple of weeks. When you're ready to use it, thaw it in the fridge overnight, bring to room temperature the next day, and use as needed.*

Garlic Paste

YIELD: 1 TABLESPOON

Ingredients:

6 garlic cloves

1 teaspoon salt

This mashed garlic, made using a mortar and pestle, is used daily in kitchens in Lebanon. I want to stress that a garlic press or simply chopping garlic is not ideal if one wants to cook Lebanese dishes. The pounding of fresh garlic with salt, resulting in a paste, is what one should go after. This mashed garlic is used in salad dressings, mezze items, soups, stews, pasta—in short, *every single dish,* especially dishes served at room temperature.

Pounding garlic into a paste was my job as an apprentice cook when I was ten years old, and my mother made me pound away until it was really smooth.Since I try not to salt too much, and there's no way to do garlic paste without the salt, I don't add it to the rest of the dish. When I add the mashed garlic to stews or soups, I do so at the end of cooking to keep the garlic fresh and pungent.

Directions:

Peel and cut the garlic cloves lengthwise; toss out the clove if it contains a green shoot, which indicates that it is old. To peel the clove easily, knock it decisively with the handle of a knife. Chop the garlic fine and place in the mortar with the salt. Pound away for 2 or 3 minutes until the mixture is the consistency of a paste. Use in cooking right away or store in the freezer, wrapped in plastic wrap and placed in an airtight container. You can prepare several such small packages at one time.

Garlic Cream *(Toom)*

YIELD: 1½ CUPS

Ingredients:

3 tablespoons cornstarch, wheat starch, or potato flour

1½ cups water

10 garlic cloves *(or more)*, finely chopped

1½ teaspoons of salt

½ cup colorless vegetable oil

1 tablespoon lemon juice

Another option shown to me by a Beiruti friend is to make a garlic cream by cooking water and flour or starch and adding the paste to the mixture. This will result in a milder garlic cream suitable as a condiment on a sandwich. This is a good option for a crowd when a lot of sandwiches are going to be passed around!

Directions:

1) Mix the starch or flour in a bowl and add the water until incorporated and the mixture is lump-free and clear. Transfer the mixture to a small saucepan over medium heat and stir gently until thickened.

2) Put the garlic in a mortar with the salt. Pound away for 4 or 5 minutes until the mixture is the consistency of a paste. Transfer the paste to a food processor, and while the machine is running, start adding the oil and lemon juice drop by drop through the feed tube. (I have found that using a colorless oil gives better results than a thick olive oil.) Transfer the garlic mixture from the food processor to the saucepan with the starch and water. Using an immersion blender, process the mixture until creamy and smooth. Cool, transfer to a bowl, and store in the fridge for up to 3 days.

Ground Meat and Onion Stuffing
(Hashwet al-Lahmeh)

The meat and onion stuffing is used to fill kibbeh balls, as a topping for pies, in stews, and as a filling for cored vegetables.

YIELD: 8 SERVINGS

Ingredients:

¼ cup oil or clarified butter

½ cup pine nuts and *(or)* sliced almonds *(or any assorted nuts)*

1 large onion, chopped

1 pound ground beef

1½ teaspoons salt

1 teaspoon allspice

¼ teaspoon cinnamon

¼ teaspoon black pepper

1 tablespoon pomegranate molasses *(optional)*

Directions:

1) Heat the oil in a skillet and fry the pine nuts or almonds until caramel-colored. Remove from the pan and place on a plate to cool.

2) Sauté the onion until soft, then add the meat, using two wooden spoons to break it up into little pieces. Sprinkle the salt, allspice, cinnamon, and pepper on the meat as it is browning. When the meat has browned, add the pomegranate molasses and stir a few seconds to combine. Set aside and cool.

3) Divide the stuffing into two freezer bags and freeze up to 2 weeks.

NOTE: *Sometimes I process the meat filling by pulsing it quickly in the food processor until the meat pieces look like tiny pellets of uniform size. Freeze the nuts in separate small bags and keep in the fridge until needed. This method will ensure that the nuts keep their crunch.*

Kafta
(Meat Paste)

Kafta is a classic Lebanese meat paste. It is used for grilled kebabs,
to stuff sandwiches, or can be made into meatballs (for a soup or stew).
Kafta is also baked in a pie pan with various toppings.

YIELD: 1½ POUNDS KAFTA PASTE

Directions:

1) Place the onion in the bowl of a food processor. Pulse a few times until it is chopped fine. Add the parsley, meat, and spices and process until the mixture is pasty.

2) Transfer to a bowl, cover and keep in the fridge till needed.

Ingredients:

1 medium onion, peeled and quartered

½ cup chopped Italian parsley

1½ pounds ground beef

1 teaspoon salt

½ teaspoon allspice

½ teaspoon cinnamon

1 teaspoon hot *(or mild)* Aleppo pepper or paprika *(optional)*

Mint Pesto (Aliiyet al-Na'na')

Mint pesto is used to flavor soups and stews as well as stuffed veggies,
such as cabbage rolls. It is an alternative to cilantro pesto.

YIELD: ¼ CUP

Ingredients:

4 tablespoons olive oil

2 tablespoons dry mint powder *(if the mint is still in leaves, crush them)*

1 tablespoon garlic paste

Directions:

Heat the oil in a skillet for a couple of minutes on medium-high heat. Add the mint powder and garlic, which should begin to sizzle. Stir with a wooden spoon for 5 seconds until the fragrance is released. Use as needed.

Nuts
(Toasted and Roasted)

Nuts are used quite frequently in Lebanese cooking (especially pine nuts), in raw form, and roasted or toasted, so having a supply on hand is a good idea. It is best to presoak nuts before roasting or toasting them. Soaking gets rid of some of the tannins and makes nuts more easily digestible, releases beneficial enzymes, makes the protein more available, and also softens them, making them more easily blended when incorporated with other ingredients. Soak them for one or two hours in water (double their volume) in a bowl.

After soaking, thoroughly rinse and dry the nuts by spreading them on paper towels or a clean kitchen towel to air dry. When dried, they can be toasted on the stove in clarified butter or oil or roasted in a 300-degree F oven for 15 minutes or until golden. They need to be closely monitored, because it takes only minutes for the nuts to burn. In Lebanese cuisine, toasting nuts is always preferred, and recently, sliced almonds have been used instead of pine nuts due to cost considerations.

Stovetop Method for Toasting Nuts:

Directions:

Heat the butter or oil in a skillet over medium heat. Add the nuts and stir until they are toasted and fragrant (about 3 minutes; smaller nuts, such as pine nuts, will be done sooner than almonds). If using an assortment of nuts, make sure to toast them separately.

Baking Method for Roasting Nuts:

If you'd rather not use butter or oil to toast nuts, you can dry-roast them in the oven. Set your oven to 350 degrees F. Spread the nuts in an even layer on a cookie sheet. Roast for 5 minutes, take them out, and move them around a bit, so they'll be roasted uniformly. Put them back in the oven, checking them every minute until they are golden brown and fragrant. Transfer them to a platter to cool.

Pine Nut Sauce

YIELD: 1 CUP or 4 to 6 SERVINGS

Ingredients:

½ cup pine nuts
  (about 2 ounces)

1 teaspoon garlic paste

2 ounces fresh bread
  crumbs *(or more)*, soaked
  briefly in water then
  squeezed dry *(or 2 slices
  American-style white
  bread, crusts removed
  and cubed)*

1 tablespoon lemon juice
  (or more to taste)

Pine Nut Sauce is a classic accompaniment to baked or fried fish. Its subtle and delicate flavor marries well with a simple baked snapper or other white-fleshed fish.

Directions:

Put all of the ingredients in the bowl of a food processor and process for a few minutes until a thick paste forms. You can add more bread crumbs (or more slices of white bread) or a little cold water or lemon juice to achieve the consistency you are after. It should be creamy like yogurt. Taste and adjust seasoning if needed. Serve cold or at room temperature with fish (grilled or baked).

NOTE: *Soak the pine nuts for one hour in water prior to using them; drain and proceed.*

Pita Croutons

YIELD: 2 CUPS

Pita croutons are used when making fattoush salad or a type of casserole called *fatteh*, as well as a dish called *treedeh*. *(See Fattoush Salad in Chapter 5 and Chickpea and Yogurt Casserole in Chapter 3.)* Making pita croutons in advance saves time and is a good way to use up leftover pita bread. They will stay crisp for at least a week.

Ingredients:

2 6–8-inch pita breads

1 cup vegetable oil

Directions:

Stovetop method:

Cut the pita breads with kitchen scissors into 1-inch-wide strips. Cut again into half-inch-wide squares. Heat the oil in a skillet and fry the croutons until golden. Remove with a slotted spoon and drain on paper towels.

Oven method:

Heat the oven to 300 degrees F. Bake for 10 minutes, until the bread is golden and crisp. Cool and then break up into bits. Keep in the turned-off oven until serving time or store in a tightly closed container.

Rice and Vermicelli Pilaf
(Ruz Bel-Sh'ariyeh)

YIELD: 4 SERVINGS

Ingredients:

¼ cup oil or clarified butter

½ cup vermicelli pasta, broken up with a meat mallet *(or your fingertips)* into 1-inch sticks

1 cup American long-grain rice (or basmati or other long-grain)

3 cups water, brought to a boil

1 teaspoon salt *(or to taste)*

This pilaf is served with most stews in the traditional Lebanese kitchen.

Directions:

1) Heat the oil or butter in a medium saucepan over medium heat. Drop the vermicelli pieces into the pan, stirring every few seconds until they are browned. Be careful—they burn quickly!

2) Add the rice and stir a minute to coat the grains in butter and to combine the rice and pasta.

3) Add the water and salt. Lower the heat and cover. Cook undisturbed for about 20 minutes. At the end of 20 minutes, lift the lid, and if you see small holes throughout the rice, it is nearly done. Set the pan aside covered and serve a few minutes later.

Salad Dressing for Everyday Use

This dressing is made daily and used with raw veggies, or boiled, stuffed veggies.

YIELD: ½ CUP PLUS 1⅓ TABLESPOONS

Ingredients:

¼ cup lemon juice

⅓ cup olive oil

1 teaspoon salt, or to taste

Directions:

Combine all ingredients in a jar or salad dressing container and shake well.

VARIATIONS: (1) Add one serving of garlic paste *(see recipe in this section)* and mix well; or (2) add 1 teaspoon sumac powder or 1 teaspoon white vinegar or sour grape vinegar (verjuice) and mix well; or (3) add 1 teaspoon pomegranate molasses. Whisk the dressing well before using.

Syrup for Arabic Pastries

YIELD: 2 CUPS

This is the basic syrup used for all desserts and pastries. A jar can be kept in the fridge in a covered jar at all times.

Directions:

In a saucepan, melt the sugar in the water over medium heat. Do not stir the mixture until it starts boiling. Skim off any froth that accumulates on the surface. Simmer the syrup for 12 minutes or so, then add the lemon juice. Test the syrup by gently placing one drop on the countertop; if it is stiff, the syrup is ready.

Ingredients:

3 cups sugar

1½ cups water

1 teaspoon fresh lemon juice

1 tablespoon orange blossom water

1 tablespoon rose water

NOTE: *If you have a candy thermometer, it can be used to determine readiness. Place the thermometer in the syrup (being sure not to rest it on the bottom of the pan). When the temperature reaches 220 degrees F, it is ready.*

Tahini and Onion Sauce
(Tagen)

YIELD: 2½ CUPS

This is a simple sauce of sautéed sliced onions, tahini, lemon juice, and water. It is called a *tagen* sauce; it can be prepared in advance and served either warm or at room temperature. It is served with fish or chicken or grilled meat. The quantities can be adjusted if you need a smaller or larger amount.

Ingredients:

3 tablespoons oil

2 large onions, sliced

1 cup water *(or enough to make the sauce creamy and smooth)*

¾ cup tahini *(always stir the jar before using)*

½ cup lemon juice *(more or less, according to taste)*

Salt, to taste

¼ cup toasted pine nuts or sliced almonds *(see "Nuts" in this chapter)*

Directions:

1) Heat the oil in a large skillet over medium heat. Add the onions, lower the heat immediately, and cover the pan for 5 minutes. Pour the water over the onions and let the mixture bubble up gently until the onions are softened and thoroughly cooked and the water is almost evaporated. Add the tahini, lemon juice, and salt, and stir for a few minutes until the oil begins to show on the surface of the sauce. Transfer the sauce to a platter, garnish with the nuts, and serve.

2) If not needed right away, transfer the sauce to a bowl, cool, and keep covered in the fridge.

Tarator Sauce

YIELD: 1 CUP

Tarator sauce is the Lebanese equivalent of mayonnaise. It is very easy and quick to prepare (it only takes five minutes), does not contain eggs, and is made with only three ingredients. It is slathered on falafel sandwiches, mixed with chick-peas for hummus, and used to dress boiled and fried vegetables, dips, and grilled meats. When making this sauce, taste as you go along, adjusting the lemon juice and the amount of garlic paste, according to taste. Some people dislike garlic and omit it when making tarator. The amount of water will be determined as you go along; it should be enough to make the sauce creamy and smooth, but not too watery.

Ingredients:

1 teaspoon garlic paste
 (see recipe p. 30)

½ cup tahini

¼ to ½ cup lemon juice
 (more or less, according to taste)

¼ to ⅓ cup water

Directions:

Place the garlic in a bowl, add the tahini, and mix well. Add the lemon juice and water gradually, stirring until the sauce is the consistency of a creamy yogurt. Add more water slowly if needed. Taste and adjust the sauce as needed.

VARIATION: Add ½ cup chopped parsley to the tarator and mix well prior to serving. This herby tarator can be used to dress salads.

Turnip Pickles *(Kabees Lefet)*

YIELD: 1 32-OUNCE JAR

Turnip pickles and cucumber pickles are inevitable trimmings for every meal in Lebanon. Every deli, coffee shop, and falafel and shawarma joint in the country adorn their shelves with tall bins of these sour and beloved pickles. These homemade ones are redder than usual, simply due to the fact that I added an extra beet in the jar. If you prefer the original light pink, just stick to one small beet per jar. These are easy to make and even easier to eat.

Ingredients:

4 cups water

1 cup coarse sea salt

2 tablespoons sugar

1½ cups red wine vinegar

1½ pounds turnips

2 small beets (*or 1, depending on if you want red or pink pickles*)

Directions:

1) Boil the water with the salt and sugar in a medium saucepan, stirring until the salt is dissolved. Remove from the heat and let cool to room temperature. Once cool, add the vinegar and stir.

2) Peel the turnips, cutting off the ends with the fibrous strings, and cut them into slices as thick as you like. Cut the beets into slices as well.

3) Start stacking the turnips in a clean, sterilized jar, nudging in a slice of beet here and there. Pour the water and vinegar mixture over the turnips and beets. Seal the jar tightly. Keep in a dark, cool, and dry cupboard for 3 weeks before opening and eating.

Walnut Sauce

YIELD: 2 CUPS

This sauce is traditionally used with grilled or broiled fish. Soaking the nuts in water for one hour prior to use is recommended to get rid of dirt and tannins. Drain and pat dry before using. This recipe was given to me by Bassem Melhem, a former resident of Beyno, a town in North Lebanon (Akkar). I had never heard of this sauce with fish and was excited to try it. Lebanon has a very regional cuisine based on what is grown in the area; in Beirut, we always served pine nut sauce with fish.

Ingredients:

1½ cups walnuts, ground into a powder in a mini food processor or coffee grinder

1 tablespoon garlic paste *(see recipe p. 30)*

½ cup lemon juice

¼ to ½ cup water

1 teaspoon salt *(or to taste)*

½ teaspoon ground chili pepper *(optional)*

Directions:

Place all the ingredients in the bowl of a mini food processor. Process until the sauce becomes somewhat smooth. Taste and adjust seasoning.

VARIATION: Another version of this sauce adds cilantro pesto *(see recipe in this chapter)*. The chopped cilantro is sautéed with the garlic paste in a bit of oil for 5 seconds until fragrant, then added to the walnut sauce. You could also add a package of frozen cilantro pesto to the sauce (reducing the amount of garlic, to taste).

Yogurt Sauce

Yogurt Sauce (Cooked)

Ingredients:

1 container *(32 ounces)* plain yogurt

½ cup cornstarch diluted in ½ cup water

1 egg whisked briefly in a bowl

1 teaspoon salt

In the traditional Lebanese kitchen, yogurt is cooked as a sauce for a stew or pasta. In order to prevent the yogurt from curdling, a cornstarch mixture is added to the yogurt broth, as well as an egg. This stabilizes the yogurt. Stir the mixture for 10 minutes and it is ready to be served with a final flourish of pesto.

Directions:

Pour the yogurt, cornstarch mixture, and egg into a saucepan. Over medium heat, stir the yogurt until steam appears. Keep stirring for at least 15 minutes until it starts bubbling. Lower the heat and let it simmer very gently for another 3 minutes or so.

Yogurt Sauce (Uncooked)

Ingredients:

4 cups plain yogurt

1 teaspoon garlic paste *(see recipe p. 30)* *(more to taste)*

Salt, to taste

4 tablespoons tahini *(optional)*

This is good to use as a sauce for pasta, boiled veggies, or casseroles (fatteh).

Directions:

Mix all the ingredients together. This keeps well in the fridge for 24 hours.

CHAPTER 3

Breads, Breakfast, and Brunch

Breakfast in Lebanon is a hearty affair.
Every neighborhood in every city or village has a
bakery churning out flatbreads (called *man'ooshe*)
in the early morning to feed a hungry crowd.
The most popular toppings are *zaatar*, cheese, or *keshek*.
In addition, a garnish of fresh sliced tomatoes,
cucumbers, olives, and mint leaves is offered as well.
Baked on-site in a large oven or on a saj,
these flatbreads keep hunger pangs
at bay for a few hours.

Yogurt Cheese *(Labneh)*

YIELD: ¾ CUP

Ingredients:

1 container *(16 ounces)*
    whole or low-fat yogurt

Extra virgin olive oil

1 teaspoon salt, or to taste

We were told that Marcel Proust loved his madeleines, because when he would bite into one, a flood of childhood memories would overtake him and he would experience bliss. I am willing to bet that for a large majority of Lebanese expats, the feeling is similar when a plate of *labneh* is presented to them.

Directions:

Line a sieve (large enough to fit the quantity of yogurt) with either a coffee filter or a paper towel. Place the sieve over a bowl, dump the yogurt into it, cover it loosely with plastic wrap, and let it sit for a minimum of 6 hours on the counter or in the refrigerator until the liquid (or "whey") is drained from the yogurt. (It is best to let it sit overnight.) The next morning, flip the drained yogurt (now labneh) onto a pretty serving dish. You can save the whey, if desired, to use in other recipes. (It can be used as a substitute for buttermilk, for making homemade ricotta, added to a smoothie for some added tang, and many other uses.) With the back of a spoon, draw a circular furrow around the inside of the drained yogurt. Pour some extra virgin olive oil into the furrow and sprinkle with salt, if desired. It is now ready! Eat labneh by scooping it up with pieces of pita. You may also wish to add fresh mint, olives, tomatoes, cucumbers, and some zaatar sprinkled on top or swirled into it.

Zaatar and Tapenade Bread

YIELD: 1 LOAF

Olives and zaatar are daily staples on the Lebanese table. Zaatar is an herb dried and mixed with sumac powder and toasted sesame seeds. I figured, why not combine olives and zaatar? The result is a moist, filled bread that goes very well with just about anything. It's perfect for breakfast with a dollop of labneh or topped with a cold cut on those nights when you want a fuss-free meal.

Ingredients:

1 batch of dough
  (see Chapter 2, "Basics")

¼ cup zaatar mix

⅓ cup olive oil
  (more or less)

1 tablespoon harissa or red pepper paste *(optional)*

1 jar *(8 ounces)* or can of olive tapenade

Directions:

1) Press down the dough after it has risen and roll it out into a large rectangle, 8 by 12 inches.

2) Mix the zaatar, oil, and harissa. Adjust the amount, if necessary, so that it forms a moist paste. Slather the paste onto the dough and then top it with the tapenade. Roll the dough into a cigar-shaped log, then coil it into a flat spiral. Place it in an oiled 9-inch round cake pan, then let it rest, undisturbed, at room temperature for at least one hour, until it has risen as much as possible.

3) Heat the oven to 375 degrees F. Bake for 35 minutes or longer, until the surface is crisp and golden. Cool, slice, and serve.

NOTE: *You can prepare this bread in advance, and let it rise in the greased cake pan in the refrigerator. Bake it until the surface is crisp and golden. Zaatar mix can be found in Middle Eastern markets. Harissa is sold in Middle Eastern stores and some main supermarkets; it is a Tunisian spicy paste served there with couscous. Any hot red pepper paste or chili paste can be substituted.*

Eggs Poached in Tomato Stew
(Beyd Bel-Banadoora)

YIELD: 4 SERVINGS

This dish always reminds me of a young man I met in the seventies in Beirut. He had to quit elementary school to help his family (his father worked in the Beirut harbor carrying shipments on his back). He had twelve siblings. We became friends and would roam the streets of old Beirut, talking nonstop about art, his writing (he wanted to become a playwright), and the cultural life in Lebanon. One day, he took me to visit his mom. The family lived in a one-room shack in a deserted lot. His mom was sitting on a folded mattress and was warm and jovial. She proceeded to make us this dish on a one-plate gas burner propped up next to her on concrete blocks. It was delicious, and we ate, using some flatbread to sop up the juices. I never forgot his mom and her courage and generosity. This dish was a dish "of the poor," but absolutely delicious.

Ingredients:

¼ cup olive oil

2 large onions, chopped fine

6 large tomatoes, skinned, seeded, and diced, with juice retained

1 tablespoon garlic paste *(see Chapter 2, "Basics")*

8 eggs

Pita bread *(or use a flatbread, such as markouk)*

Directions:

1) Heat the oil in a large skillet over medium heat for 5 minutes. Add the onions and sauté until golden and soft, about 15 minutes.

2) Add the tomatoes with their juice. Heat the mixture gently for 10 minutes.

3) Stir in the garlic paste, distributing it throughout, and heat for an additional 5 minutes.

4) Break an egg into a small custard bowl. Using a wooden spoon, carve out a large opening in the tomato and onion mixture. Drop the egg into it. Proceed with the second egg and so on. Cook on top of the stove for about 15 minutes, until the whites are set.

Eggs with Potato
(Mfarket el-Batata)

YIELD: 4 SERVINGS

This is the quintessential Lebanese mountain dish. It is prepared with seasonal vegetables and some fresh eggs.

Directions:

1) Put the potatoes in a large bowl and cover them with water. Set aside.

2) Heat the oils in a large skillet over medium heat.

3) Drain the water from the potatoes, pat them dry, and add them to the skillet. Fry until golden. Remove the potatoes from the skillet, draining them of most of the oil, and place them into another skillet.

4) Whisk the eggs, salt, pepper, and allspice together in a bowl, then pour them onto the potatoes and set the skillet on medium-low heat. When the eggs are set, serve.

Ingredients:

2 large potatoes, peeled and diced

1½ cups olive oil

1½ cups corn oil

8 eggs

1 teaspoon salt *(or to taste)*

½ teaspoon ground white pepper

½ teaspoon ground allspice

NOTE: *The leftover oil can be strained, transferred into a jar, sealed, and kept in the fridge (or freezer) for more uses.*

Oven-Baked Omelet with Parsley and Onion *(Ejjeh)*

YIELD: 4 SERVINGS

Ingredients:

8 large eggs

1 cup chopped Italian parsley

1 medium onion, chopped

¼ cup all-purpose flour

Salt, to taste

Pinch of ground black or white pepper

Pinch of ground cinnamon

4 tablespoons olive oil

This rustic omelet is ubiquitous in Lebanese mountain villages, where it is made with a handful of home-grown parsley and onion.

Directions:

1) Preheat the oven to 350 degrees F. In a bowl, beat the eggs with the parsley, onion, flour, salt, pepper, and cinnamon.

2) Pour the oil into an ovenproof omelet platter and heat for 5 minutes. Pour the egg mixture into the platter all at once. Immediately transfer to the oven and bake for 15 minutes or until the omelet has puffed up and is set.

3) When the omelet is set, remove and serve warm or at room temperature with pita bread, pickles, and/or sliced tomatoes on the side.

Fava Bean Soup *(Ful Mudammas)*

YIELD: 4 SERVINGS

Ful (pronounced "fool") is Egypt's and Lebanon's food of the common folk, usually prepared by street vendors who cook it in huge cauldrons from the afternoon until the next day, when it becomes meltingly tender. "Ful" is the name for fava beans, as well as the dish made of cooked fava beans. It is an ancient food that some people claim was eaten by the pharaohs and certainly their subjects.

Ful is extremely easy to prepare. The cans of ful made in Lebanon and distributed overseas have a mixture of chickpeas and fava beans. You can buy cans of prepared ful mudammas in Middle Eastern stores and then doctor them as you like, or you can cook the fava beans and chickpeas from scratch. Ful, once tender, is garnished with diced tomatoes, onions, parsley, lemon juice, garlic, and olive oil. It is served with pickles, cucumbers, and bread.

Ingredients:

2 cans *(15.5 ounces)*
  ful mudammas
  (with chickpeas)

2 teaspoons garlic paste
  (see Chapter 2, "Basics")

1 large lemon, juiced
  *(about 3 or 4 tablespoons;
  may substitute lime or
  Seville orange juice)*

½ cup olive oil

½ cup finely chopped
  parsley

Pita bread

Trimmings: Sliced
  radishes, diced tomatoes,
  chopped onions, diced
  jalapeño peppers
  (optional), hard-boiled
  eggs.

Directions:

1) Drain the liquid from the ful mudammas and put them in a saucepan. Fill the empty cans with fresh tap water and pour into the saucepan along with the beans. Cook for 15 minutes or longer over low to medium heat.

2) Once the beans are warmed, use an immersion blender (or a meat mallet) to mash one third of the beans and cook a bit longer until the soup gets very thick.

3) Add the garlic paste, lemon juice, oil, and parsley, and stir to combine; taste and adjust seasoning to your liking. Serve with pita bread and your choice of trimmings.

Zaatar Flatbread
(Man'ooshet Zaatar)

YIELD: 6 FLATBREADS

A Lebanese blogger ran a popular post once that reviewed all the zaatar flatbreads (man'ooshes) made in the city's neighborhood bakeries. He enlisted a dozen friends to scout all the different bakeries in order to find the best ones. Luckily, the one bakery with the highest marks was down the street from my apartment. Unfortunately, most of us who live overseas do not have a neighborhood bakery a few feet away that delivers fresh zaatar man'ooshe. The solution is to make a monthly supply and freeze them in individual portions (for up to four weeks). Zaatar man'ooshes will quickly recover their fresh taste once warmed up in the oven.

Ingredients:

1 batch turnover dough
 (see Chapter 2, "Basics")

1½ cups zaatar mix
 (more as needed)

2 cups olive oil *(add more
 as needed to make a paste)*

Trimmings:

Sliced tomatoes, cucumbers, olives, and fresh mint leaves are usually offered with this flatbread, as well as yogurt cheese (labneh).

Directions for oven-baked zaatar:

1) Heat the oven to 375 degrees F. On a floured work surface, roll the dough into the size of your choice. To make small happy hour–size flatbreads, roll out the dough and cut circles with a 4-inch cookie cutter. Place the circles on a cookie sheet lined with parchment paper.

2) Mix the zaatar with the oil in a small bowl until it is the consistency of a paste.

3) Cover the top of the dough circles with the zaatar paste. Bake for 7 minutes until golden and crisp. (If you're making pizza-size flatbreads, roll the dough into a long 15-inch sausage and divide it into 6 equal parts. Roll out each section into a circle, cover with zaatar paste, and bake for about 15 minutes at 375 degrees F.)

Zaatar-topped flatbreads will keep in the freezer for up to four weeks, tightly sealed; reheat gently in a 325-degree F oven for 10 minutes or so. It is best to freeze them rather than keep them in the fridge, as they dry out quickly.

NOTE: *When rolling out each dough circle, it is easier to do so on a piece of parchment paper. Zaatar mix can be found in Middle Eastern groceries.*

Chickpea and Yogurt Casserole
(Fattet al-Hummus)

YIELD: 4 SERVINGS

This rustic dish is traditional in Lebanese cooking. It is prepared in hole-in-the-wall eateries that serve it as early as 6:00 AM to throngs of workers. It is easy to prepare and delicious.

Ingredients:

2 cans *(15.5 ounces)* chickpeas

2 cups water

4 cups pita croutons
(see Chapter 2, "Basics")

1 recipe uncooked yogurt sauce *(see Chapter 2, "Basics")*

3 tablespoons fried pine nuts *(or almond slices; see "Nuts" in Chapter 2, "Basics")*

Pomegranate arils to garnish *(optional)*

1 teaspoon ground cumin

Directions:

1) Drain the liquid from the chickpeas and put them in a saucepan. Add the water and set the pan on medium-low heat. Simmer the chickpeas for at least 15 minutes (or longer, up to 45 minutes) until they are meltingly tender.

2) Place the pita croutons in the bottom of a serving dish. Transfer the chickpeas with a half ladle of the cooking water onto the croutons. Pour the yogurt sauce over the heated chickpeas. Garnish with the pine nuts and pomegranate arils. Sprinkle with cumin and serve the dish immediately.

NOTE: *The pomegranate is not traditional, just a fun touch. The pita croutons are sometimes fried in clarified butter, which increases their taste tenfold but also adds calories.*

Taro in Citrus-Tahini Sauce
(Kolkass Bel-Arnabiyeh)

YIELD: 4 SERVINGS

Taro is a vegetable similar to a potato and is grown locally in Lebanon. It can be found in most supermarkets in North America. It is supposed to be even more nutritious than potatoes. The only drawback is that peeling it is a bit annoying. One method consists in boiling it whole for five minutes, then peeling it. In Middle Eastern stores, taro (or *kolkass*) is imported from Egypt and can be found in the freezer section, already cut up with a seasoning packet. This dish can be prepared with cauliflower instead of taro, using the same parboiling technique (believed to rid the vegetable of its annoying, gas-producing properties).

This dish, with a citrus-tahini sauce, is a Lebanese creation. It really takes the tahini flavor of the sauce to new heights with the combination of different citruses. Raji Kibbé, owner of one of the oldest and best ful stands in Beirut, freezes all his citrus juices while their fruit is in season in order to make his sauce for his *msabbaha* (same dish with chickpeas). Otherwise, this dish can be prepared with a medley of seasonal fresh citrus.

Ingredients:

1 pound taro root

1 teaspoon lemon juice or vinegar

3 cups citrus-tahini sauce *(see Chapter 2, "Basics")*

1 can *(15.5 ounces)* cooked chickpeas

Salt, to taste

¼ cup fried or roasted pine nuts or almonds *(see "Nuts" in Chapter 2, "Basics")*

3 cups vegetable oil *(optional)*

Directions

1) In a deep pot, boil the taro root for 5 minutes. Drain, peel, and cut into chunks. Put the chunks in a bowl and cover them with water. Add the lemon juice (or vinegar). Soak the chunks for at least 10 minutes, then drain.

2) Put the citrus-tahini sauce in a large saucepan over medium-low heat and stir for a few minutes. Add the taro chunks and cook in the sauce for about 30 minutes.

3) Halfway through, rinse and drain the chickpeas and add them to the taro. Simmer the mixture until the taro chunks are cooked through. Salt to taste and serve, garnished with nuts if desired.

NOTE: *If you're not concerned about calories, after draining the taro chunks, dry them and fry them in a hot oil bath until golden, then finish cooking them in the sauce (traditional).*

Zaatar and Yogurt Cheese Hand Pies

YIELD: 12 HAND PIES

A traditional Lebanese breakfast? Pinching off pieces of pita bread, scooping up some zaatar (marinated in olive oil) and yogurt cheese (labneh), and adding some chopped tomatoes and mint. Well, here is a dish that is half the work—a pie containing the zaatar in olive oil and the labneh. The dough I have used is called *sambusek* and is the equivalent of an American hand pie.

Directions:

1) Mix the flour, salt, sugar, and baking powder in a medium-size bowl until well combined. Add the butter and ¼ cup of the oil and cut it into the flour using your fingertips or a couple of forks until the butter is no longer visible. Add a bit of water and mix until a dough forms. Wrap the dough in plastic and set it in the fridge for 30 minutes.

2) Preheat the oven to 375 degrees F. Roll out the dough as thin as possible and cut it into 4-inch circles. In a medium-size bowl, mix the zaatar and remaining oil until it forms a paste. Add the yogurt cheese and onions to the zaatar paste and mix until well combined.

3) Place 1 tablespoon of the mixture in the middle of the dough circles. Sprinkle a few olives on top, and any other filling ingredients you desire. Fold the dough over the filling, pinching the edges tight so the filling won't leak out during baking. Set the stuffed hand pies gently on a baking sheet lined with parchment paper. Bake the pies for 12 minutes or until they are golden and dry. Serve warm or at room temperature with sliced tomatoes, cucumbers, and fresh mint leaves on the side, if desired.

NOTE: *Zaatar mix can be found in Middle Eastern groceries.*

Dough:

2 cups all-purpose flour *(can combine with ½ cup whole wheat flour or some wheat or oat bran)*

1 teaspoon salt

1 teaspoon sugar

½ teaspoon baking powder

4 tablespoons clarified butter *(more if needed) (see Chapter 2, "Basics")*

¾ cup olive oil

⅓ cup water *(or more, as needed)*

Filling:

3 tablespoons zaatar mix *(more to taste)*

2 cups yogurt cheese *(see Chapter 2, "Basics")*

1 small white onion, chopped

⅓ cup chopped green or black olives *(optional)*

⅓ cup other filling ingredients as desired, such as chopped dried tomatoes, diced red bell peppers, or cherry tomatoes

Turnovers with Purslane, Tomato, and Onion Salad
(Fatayer Be-Salatet al-Bakleh)

YIELD: 6 LARGE TURNOVERS

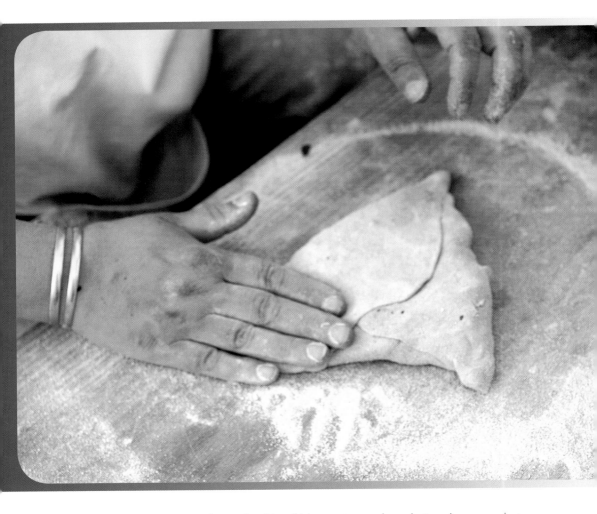

These turnovers are popular in the Chouf Mountains and made in a large pocket-size (one makes a serving). The veggies are dressed with sumac, lemon juice, and olive oil. This is a rustic, healthy, and delightful savory pastry with the tang of sumac and the crunch of onions.

Directions:

1) Put the filling ingredients into a bowl and marinate in the marinade mixture for 30 minutes.

2) While the filling is marinating, shape the dough into a long sausage about 15 inches long; cut into 6 pieces. Roll each piece into a circle, lightly brush with a touch of oil, and place on a greased baking sheet.

3) Preheat the oven to 375 degrees F.

4) Using a sieve or a colander, drain the marinade from the filling (the marinade can be saved to use as a salad dressing for other meals). Place 1 cup or so of the filling onto the middle of each dough circle and fold the dough over the filling, pinching the three edges together to prevent the filling from coming out during baking. The turnover will look like a giant triangle.

5) Brush the top of the turnovers with olive oil for a crispier crust if desired. Bake for 15 minutes or until the turnovers are golden and dry. Serve warm or at room temperature.

Ingredients:

Filling:

3 bunches purslane (or baby spinach or baby arugula), chopped coarsely

2 medium white onion, chopped fine

6 medium tomatoes, chopped fine

1 cup chopped Italian parsley

1 cup chopped green bell pepper, if desired

2 tablespoon dry mint powder

Marinade:

⅓ cup olive oil

¼ cup lemon juice

2 tablespoons sumac

Salt, to taste

Dough:

1 recipe turnover dough (see recipe in "Basics")

NOTE: *Adding a few bits of feta cheese to this turnover would be a welcome addition.*

Sfoof Pancakes

YIELD: 12 TO 15 PANCAKES

Sfoof is a cake that used to be sold by street-cart vendors all over the streets of Beirut. Today it is mostly found in Arabic pastry shops, as the street carts are fast disappearing from the landscape of the city. The distinct feature of this bread is its yellow color, a result of the turmeric. I've created a pancake version with the same flavors, and truth be told, I like this a lot better than the traditional cake version. The turmeric and anise add an exotic touch to the pancakes, and the syrup gives it a moistness that is lacking in the cake (especially after it has been on display for a few hours outside).

Directions:

1) Preheat the oven to 175 degrees F. In a small bowl, whisk together the flour, semolina, sugar, baking powder, salt, anise, and turmeric; set aside.

2) In a medium-size bowl, whisk together the milk, butter or oil, and egg.

3) Add the dry ingredients to the milk mixture. Whisk until just moistened.

4) Heat a large nonstick skillet over medium heat and oil it with cooking spray or a piece of oiled wax paper.

5) For each pancake, spoon 2 to 3 tablespoons of batter onto the skillet, using the back of the spoon to spread the batter into a round shape. Cook until bubbles appear on the surface of the pancakes and a few have burst, 1 to 2 minutes. Sprinkle each pancake with 2 or 3 pine nuts (before the batter dries up). Flip and cook until browned on the other side, 1 to 2 minutes more.

6) Transfer the pancakes to an ovenproof plate, cover loosely with aluminum foil, and keep warm in the oven. Serve with syrup or honey.

Ingredients:

1 cup all-purpose flour

½ cup fine semolina *(may substitute polenta)*

¼ cup granulated sugar

1 teaspoon baking powder

½ teaspoon salt

½ teaspoon ground anise

1 teaspoon ground turmeric

1 cup milk

4 tablespoons melted unsalted butter or vegetable oil

1 large egg

1 tablespoon vegetable oil

¼ cup pine nuts *(or sliced almonds; pine nuts are more traditional)*

Syrup *(see Chapter 2, "Basics")* or honey

NOTE: *If you want the pancakes to be identical, even-shaped rounds, pour the batter into a greased cookie cutter on the skillet.*

Semolina Cheesecake
(Knefeh Bel-Jeben)

YIELD: 8 SERVINGS

This cheesecake is a widely popular breakfast item. Neighborhood pastry shops usually prepare it, however, this recipe is easy to make at home. The only caveat is that the cheese needs to be desalted. To do this, cut the cheese into slices, place it in a bowl covered with tap water for 15 minutes, and then drain the water, refilling with fresh water. Continue this operation for a couple of hours or until no taste of salt remains. Drain the cheese thoroughly on paper towels. A good cheese for this cake is a fresh mozzarella or *akkawi*, its Lebanese equivalent, or one called sweet cheese, which is sold at Arab grocers specifically to make this cake.

Ingredients:

3 cups semolina *(fine or a mixture of coarse and fine)*

1 teaspoon active dry yeast

1 cup clarified butter

1 cup whole milk

2 tablespoons orange blossom water *(or you may substitute rose water)*

2 pounds akkawi *(sweet cheese)* or desalted fresh mozzarella *(see note below)*

Syrup *(see Chapter 2, "Basics")*

Directions:

1) Mix the semolina, yeast and butter in a mixing bowl. Add the milk and orange blossom water and mix until a dough forms. Cover the bowl and set aside overnight.

2) Preheat the oven to 375 degrees F. Spray or line a 9" or 10" baking pan with parchment paper. Divide the dough in half and spread one half over the bottom of the pan. Cover the surface with the cheese slices. Cover the cheese with the remaining dough.

3) Bake the cheesecake about 25 minutes or until golden brown. Serve warm with syrup.

NOTE: *If the dough is too stiff, moisten it with a few drops of orange blossom water and knead it for a few minutes until it becomes malleable.*

Flatbread with Keshek
(Man'ooshet Keshek)

YIELD: 6 FLATBREADS (OR MORE DEPENDING ON SIZE)

Ingredients:

1 batch dough
 (see Chapter 2, "Basics")

1¼ cup olive oil *(more if
 needed to make a thick but
 moist paste)*

4 Roma tomatoes, diced
 (or ½ cup tomato sauce)

1 small onion, chopped
 very fine

1 cup keshek

1 teaspoon salt, or to taste

1 green bell pepper, seeded
 and diced small *(optional)*

1 teaspoon chili powder,
 ground paprika, or hot
 Aleppo pepper *(optional)*

½ cup walnuts, chopped
 fine *(optional)*

¼ cup sesame seeds, lightly
 toasted *(optional)*

This flatbread is offered every morning in every neighborhood bakery *(furn)* in Lebanon. This is a standard keshek recipe used for flatbreads. Make it in cocktail-size pieces for a mezze or happy hour, to take to the beach, or for a picnic.

Directions:

1) Preheat the oven to 350 degrees F. Punch down the risen ball of dough and separate it into 6 balls. Flour each ball and place it on a floured tray. On a floured work surface, roll out one ball at a time to about ¼-inch thickness. Place on a baking sheet lined with parchment paper.

2) In a small bowl, mix the oil, tomatoes (or tomato sauce), onion, keshek, salt, and any of the optional toppings that you favor.

3) As a precaution, before spreading the filling over each flatbread, pinch a ridge around the edges of the dough circles to help prevent the filling from trickling onto the baking sheet or oven floor while baking.

4) Spread one sixth of the filling on top of each of the flatbreads. Bake for about 10 minutes or until the flatbreads are golden and dry. Serve.

NOTE: *Some bakeries in Beirut add diced green bell pepper to the topping, a very pleasant variation. The chili powder, walnuts, and sesame seeds are added in some rural mountain areas.*

CHAPTER 4

Sandwiches and Soups

Sandwiches in Lebanon are made with pita bread,
which is half as thin as the pita breads found in the U.S.
Many Lebanese children are sent off to school
with a pita bread sandwich rolled and filled with yogurt
cheese, sliced tomatoes and cucumbers, and a drizzle of
olive oil. The only other traditional sandwiches are
the shawarma ones on the rotating spit, made to order,
with either beef or chicken and falafel.
Soups are often associated with religious holidays
or communities. Lentil soup, flavored with cilantro pesto,
is a big favorite; the boost of flavor from the
cilantro pesto, coupled with a squeeze of fresh
lemon juice, is the best winter soup I know of.

Yogurt Cheese and Veggie Roll-Ups
(Arooss Labneh)

YIELD: 1 ROLL-UP

Arooss labneh is the quintessential sandwich that every Lebanese kid remembers taking to school in the morning or eating upon returning home in the afternoon. I have even seen grown-ups go wild for this labneh roll-up. Whenever we had friends or relatives visit Lebanon, I'd take them on the obligatory tour of the main landmarks. Baalbek, an extraordinary site of Roman temples, was an absolute no-miss: the tour bus would stop in Chtaura, a town right before Baalbek, where a string of sandwich shops serve labneh with homemade bread from a famous dairy farm nearby. Throngs of people would hurl themselves out of the bus and storm the deli, barking orders for that sandwich—"Get me a labneh sandwich!"—as if they had been starved for days.

Ingredients:

Pita bread

½ cup yogurt cheese
  (see recipe on p. 56)

¼ cup olives

1 tomato, sliced

1 cucumber, sliced

6 fresh mint leaves or
  ½ tablespoon dry
  powdered mint

2 tablespoons olive oil

Directions:

Open one pita bread and slather the yogurt cheese on it. Scatter the olives, tomato, cucumber, and mint on top and drizzle with the olive oil. Roll up and serve. This recipe is for an 8-inch pita; increase the amount of cheese if the pita is larger or to taste.

Sandwiches

Grilled Chicken Sandwich
(Sheesh Tawook)

YIELD: 4 SERVINGS

This sandwich, called *sheesh tawook* sandwich in Lebanon, is what my son and his friends lived on *all summer* while vacationing in the Chouf Mountains. This sandwich is made up of pieces of seasoned chicken chunks. The chicken can be baked, grilled, or panfried. It is served with a coating of garlic cream (called *toom*), a few french fries, and a few pickles, and is rolled up in a large pita. In Lebanon, butcher shops sell the chicken already seasoned so all one needs to do is bake it in the oven for a few minutes. When seasoning the chicken yourself, it is best to marinate it overnight.

The night before:

In a large bowl, whisk the marinade ingredients together to combine. Add the chicken, making sure each piece is coated. Place in an ovenproof casserole dish, cover with plastic wrap, and refrigerate overnight.

Directions:

1) Heat the oven to 350 degrees F. Remove the plastic wrap from the casserole dish and bake the chicken with the marinade for 10 minutes. Bake the fries at the same time as the chicken. (If you prefer, you may panfry the chicken in a skillet with the french fries instead.)

2) Drain the marinade (you may reserve it and freeze it to recycle later if you like) and broil the chicken until nice brown spots appear here and there.

3) Split open one pita and slather one side with garlic cream. Place a few chicken pieces on the pita, add some french fries and a few pickles, and sprinkle with some parsley. Roll it up using a piece of aluminum foil or kitchen paper to hold it tight and serve immediately with the trimmings on the side.

NOTE: *Although ketchup is widely used in this marinade, it can be replaced by tomato paste or tomato puree. Some prefer to substitute plain yogurt instead of ketchup. To save time, use a spice mix for the chicken, which is available in all Middle Eastern stores.*

Ingredients:

1 pound boneless chicken breasts, cut into chunks and marinated overnight

Marinade for the chicken:

½ cup lemon juice

1 tablespoon vinegar *(apple cider, white wine, or rice)*

½ cup olive oil

1 onion, pureed in a blender

1 tablespoon garlic paste *(see Chapter 2, "Basics")*

½ cup ketchup *(see note below)*

1 teaspoon salt, to taste

½ teaspoon ground white pepper

1 teaspoon ground Aleppo pepper *(or paprika)* or chili powder

½ teaspoon ground nutmeg

½ teaspoon ground cinnamon

Filling:

1 cup garlic cream *(see Chapter 2, "Basics")*

2 cups french fries *(frozen or fresh)*, panfried *(or baked)*

Pickles

½ cup chopped Italian parsley

4 pitas *(more as needed)*

Trimmings:

Radishes in a bowl of ice water, sliced tomatoes, olives, cucumbers, and/or sliced green bell peppers

Sandwiches

Kafta Sandwich

YIELD: 4 SERVINGS

The idea behind this sandwich is speed and convenience. The meat paste *(kafta)* can be prepared in minutes with a food processor. It can also be made in advance *(see Basics, p. 33)*, refrigerated, and used later. Kafta is slathered on pitas, quickly baked and savored as a delicious sandwich with all the trimmings.

Directions:

1) Sprinkle the chopped onions with the salt, all spice, cinnamon, and pepper, and toss a bit to combine; set aside for 15 minutes while you prepare the topping ingredients. Squeeze the onions dry and place them in the bowl of a food processor. Add the meat and ½ cup of the parsley. Process for 3 minutes or until the mixture turns pasty and smooth. Transfer to a bowl.

2) Preheat the oven to 350 degrees F and line a baking sheet with foil. Using a spatula, smear one quarter of the tomato paste on top of each of the pitas, then smear one quarter of the meat paste on top of the tomato paste, spreading it as evenly as possible. Place on the baking sheet and bake for 7 minutes or so, or until the meat is cooked.

3) Remove from the oven and serve open-faced, topped with the sliced onions, the remaining parsley, the sumac, and other topping ingredients (tomatoes, peppers, and pickles).

VARIATION: The topping ingredients could be dressed with lemon juice, olive oil, salt, and pepper.

Ingredients:

2 small onions, 1 chopped, the other sliced in rings for garnish

1 teaspoon salt

½ teaspoon ground allspice

½ teaspoon ground cinnamon

1 teaspoon hot *(or mild)* ground Aleppo pepper or ground paprika *(optional)*

¾ pound ground beef

1 cup finely chopped Italian parsley

½ cup tomato paste *(more if needed)*

4 pitas *(around 8 inches)*

Topping:

2 tablespoons sumac

1 cup cherry tomatoes *(or 1 large tomato, sliced)*

1 bell pepper, seeded and diced

1 cup pickles *(optional)*

Sandwiches

Beef Shawarma Sandwich

YIELD: 8 SERVINGS

Beef (and chicken) shawarma roasting on a spit is a ubiquitous sight in Beirut, or any village in Lebanon. It is an Ottoman legacy of more than four hundred years of the Turkish power controlling the region.

The shawarma spit rotating continuously with the flames licking the meat slices spurs the appetite of passers-by. The meat is kept moist by virtue of a large piece of lamb tail fat (called *leeyeh*), strategically placed at the very top. When the fat melts, it drips on the meat, keeping it basted with fat. Lamb tail fat is sold in butcher shops in Lebanon, just as lard is sold in North America. To prepare shawarma at home, marinate the meat overnight in a special mixture of spices. At serving time, fry or bake the meat slices rapidly and assemble the sandwich with all the trimmings in minutes. It is far easier to bake the seasoned meat slices (they will cook in minutes in a 350-degree F oven), topped with sliced tomatoes and onions.

Directions:

1) Place the meat in the freezer for about 30 minutes to make it easier to cut into small pieces (or use an electric knife). Cut the meat into thin and long pieces (about 2 inches long and ⅓ inch wide) and place in a bowl with the onion and garlic. Add the shawarma spice mix and toss to combine. Whisk the vinegar and oil and add it to the bowl. Cover and refrigerate for 24 hours (or longer).

2) *To panfry:* Remove the meat from the bowl and dry it on paper towels. Reserve the marinade.

3) Heat the lard, bacon fat, or oil in a large skillet over medium heat for 5 minutes. Add the meat and panfry for 3 to 5 minutes.

4) *To bake:* Preheat the oven to 350 degrees F. Drain the meat and put it in an ovenproof pan. Top with the sliced tomatoes and onions and ¾ cup of the reserved marinade. Bake in a preheated 350-degree F oven for 15 minutes or until cooked.

5) Split open the first pita and insert several meat slices, tomato slices, pickles, and a generous dollop of tarator sauce. Proceed with the other sandwiches.

Ingredients:

2 pounds meat *(use lamb fillet or beef sirloin)*

2 medium onions, grated or chopped fine

1 tablespoon garlic paste

⅓ cup shawarma spices *(either from ready-made spice mix or read suggested list below)*

¾ cup red wine vinegar

¾ cup olive oil

½ cup lard, bacon fat, or olive oil

8 pita breads *(or more, as needed)*

6 medium tomatoes, sliced

Pickles

2 cups tarator sauce *(see Chapter 2, "Basics")*

Shawarma spices:

½ teaspoon black pepper, 1 teaspoon cinnamon, 1 teaspoon allspice, 1 teaspoon cardamom, ½ teaspoon nutmeg, and 5 mastic pebbles ground with a dash of salt in a small mortar until powdery. These spices are mixed in a small bowl and added to the marinade.

Sandwiches

Po'boy Sandwich, Lebanese-Style

YIELD: 4 SERVINGS

This delicious Po'boy sandwich can be put together quickly with a supply of shredded cabbage and a bowl of tarator sauce from the fridge. The crisp cabbage smothered in the lemony and garlicky tarator pairs well with the smooth creaminess of the fish fillet. Wrapped in a pita roll, it is an ideal sandwich any day!

Ingredients:

1 pound white fish fillets

4 tablespoons olive oil

1 teaspoon salt, or to taste

2 teaspoons ground cumin *(optional)*

Pinch ground white pepper

1 teaspoon ground paprika or chili powder

½ cup chopped parsley

2 lemons, sliced thin

2 cups shredded white cabbage

1 cup tarator sauce *(see Chapter 2, "Basics")*

4 pita breads

1 cup chopped pickles

Directions:

1) Heat the oven to 350 degrees F. Place the fillets on a cookie sheet sprayed with cooking oil. Brush them with the oil and sprinkle them with salt, cumin, pepper, and paprika. Sprinkle parsley on top of the fillets and cover them with the lemon slices. Bake for 12 minutes or until done. Transfer to a platter and break apart into chunks.

2) Mix the cabbage and tarator sauce in a bowl.

3) Open each pita and fill with the fish chunks and cabbage and sauce. Add bits of pickles if desired. Roll up and serve.

Sandwiches

Falafel Sandwich

YIELD: 40 TO 50 FALAFELS

This humble street food, born in Egypt (where it is called *ta'amiyah*), has traveled quite a distance—first to Lebanon (where it is called falafel) and Syria, and now to the Western world. I suspect our Lebanese forefathers who fled to Egypt during the Ottoman period may have brought it back home to Lebanon. In any case, the Lebanese version differs from the Egyptian one in that the Lebanese falafel contains chickpeas in paste.

I recommend using a meat grinder to make a smooth falafel dough, otherwise a food processor will do. Falafel molds, which ensure uniform patties, are sold in all Middle Eastern stores. A cookie dough or ice-cream scoop is fine to use instead (or a tablespoon), if you don't have a mold.

Taste of Beirut

Directions:

1) Drain the beans and chickpeas and spread them flat on a towel to dry. Put them in a meat grinder and run through once. (If you don't have a meat grinder, pulse the beans and chickpeas in a food processor until well ground.)

2) Add the spices, herbs, and flour and run through the meat grinder (or food processor) again. The dough should be smooth and a bit sticky. Place the dough in a bowl, cover, and put in the fridge.

3) In a deep pot, heat the oil to 375 degrees F. Remove the dough from the fridge, add the baking powder and baking soda, and mix well. Shape the falafel patties, gently drop them into the hot oil. Fry on both sides until golden brown. Remove the falafel with a slotted spoon and drain on a paper towel–lined plate. Serve immediately with the tarator sauce and trimmings.

NOTE: *The falafel patties can be frozen prior to frying and used as desired. Some people like to add an egg to the dough, though I'd only try this if you are planning to make the falafel right away. To save time, use a couple of tablespoons of falafel spices instead of the spices in the ingredients list. They can be found in any Middle Eastern store or online. If you are planning to make falafel and kibbeh a lot, I'd recommend investing in a meat grinder; the texture obtained through this appliance cannot be duplicated in a food processor. The food processor is just a satisfactory option, not the best.*

Ingredients:

1½ cups yellow dried fava beans and ½ cup chickpeas, soaked overnight in cold water

1 tablespoon ground cumin

2 teaspoons dried coriander

1 teaspoon salt

1 teaspoon ground hot Aleppo pepper or chili powder

½ teaspoon ground cinnamon

½ teaspoon ground black pepper

1 large onion, chopped

1 large leek, chopped (*discard the fibrous tip*), or 3 scallions

2 cups cilantro, chopped

2 cups Italian parsley, chopped

2 tablespoons garlic paste

1 tablespoon flour or fine bulgur

Oil bath (*6 cups of vegetable oil*)

2 teaspoons baking powder

1 teaspoon baking soda

Tarator sauce (*see Chapter 2, "Basics"*), for serving

Trimmings:

Pita bread, pickles, sliced tomatoes, fresh mint and radishes, baby arugula

Sandwiches

Roasted Cauliflower and Potato Sandwich

YIELD: 4 SANDWICHES

The idea for this sandwich came to me after I spent time at a major food exhibit in Beirut geared to restaurants and hotels. One of the most popular stands was a shawarma chain with American-inspired merchandising (salads in boxes to shake, and other such gimmicks). I read their menu and saw a cauliflower shawarma and a potato shawarma sandwich. What a perfect choice for a vegetarian! The following week I tried both versions. This is a home version of the two sandwiches combined.

Directions:

1) Heat the oven to 375 degrees F. Line a baking sheet with aluminum foil and spray with cooking spray.

2) Break the cauliflower into florets and place on the baking sheet. Place the french fries alongside the cauliflower florets. Douse in the oil and sprinkle with the salt, Aleppo pepper or paprika, and black pepper. Roast in the oven until the florets have brown spots and the fries are soft and crispy, about 20 minutes. Toss the cauliflower gently during the baking process to make sure it gets roasted all over.

1) Open a pita and place some of the florets and a few French fries on the bread, add some tarator sauce, a few tomato slices, and pickles, and sprinkle with parsley. Roll up and serve.

Ingredients:

½ head cauliflower, boiled briefly for 4 minutes in salted boiling water, then drained thoroughly

2 cups frozen french fries *(ready to bake)*

1 cup olive oil *(or a combo of olive oil and vegetable oil)*

1 teaspoon salt

1 teaspoon ground mild or hot Aleppo pepper or paprika *(optional)*

½ teaspoon black pepper

4 pita breads *(more as needed; Lebanese pita bread is larger in size)*

1 cup tarator sauce *(see Chapter 2, "Basics")*

4 tomatoes, sliced

2 cups sliced pickles *(cucumber)*

½ cup chopped Italian parsley, for garnish

NOTE: *The veggies can be fried instead of roasted, which would improve their flavor immensely (though it does add calories). After parboiling the cauliflower, drain it, cut it into florets, and fry it in a skillet with the potatoes. The cauliflower is boiled first due to a belief among Lebanese cooks that this step will reduce its gas-inducing properties.*

Sandwiches

Lentil Soup with Swiss Chard
(Adass Bel-Hamud)

YIELD: 4 SERVINGS

Lentil soups are very popular in Lebanon. This one is traditional, rustic, and hearty. It is the perfect antidote for a cold when one feels the need for strength. It is made with the large green lentils sold in every supermarket across the United States. It was my favorite soup growing up—and my daughter's as well—and remains so today.

Directions:

Heat the oil in a soup pot and sauté the onions until golden. Add the lentils to the pot with the water or stock. Simmer until the lentils are cooked, about 45 minutes. Add the chard or greens to the soup immediately and simmer 10 minutes longer. Add the cilantro pesto the last 3 minutes of cooking, stirring to combine. Add the lemon juice to the soup. Serve warm, offering lemon quarters to squeeze more fresh lemon juice into one's individual bowl as desired.

Ingredients:

3 tablespoons olive oil

1 large onion, chopped *(about 1 cup)*

1 cup green lentils

6 cups water or veggie stock

1 bunch Swiss chard *(may substitute kale, radish greens, turnip greens, or spinach), chopped*

1 package cilantro pesto *(see Chapter 2, "Basics")*

3 medium lemons *(2 juiced and one quartered) (about ⅓ cup juice)*

VARIATIONS: This soup has many versions. Some like to add a cup of elbow pasta the last ten minutes of cooking; others like to add diced potatoes or zucchini. The greens can be split into stalks and leaves, with the stalks recycled into a dip *(see recipe in Chapter 5)*.

Soups

Mixed Vegetable Soup
(Shorbet al-Khudra)

YIELD: 8 SERVINGS

A light and healthful soup prepared with a medley of leftover vegetables.

Directions:

Put the meat, cinnamon stick, bay leaf, pepper, salt, and water in a Dutch oven. Bring to a simmer, skimming the froth from the surface of the soup until it no longer appears. Add the tomatoes, carrots, zucchinis, leeks, onions, celery, potatoes, parsley, cinnamon, and allspice, and simmer for one hour longer until all the vegetables are cooked. Add the pasta the last 10 minutes of cooking. A drizzle of olive oil and a tablespoon of garlic paste can be added the last 10 minutes for a fresh kick of flavor.

NOTE: *The soup can be pureed with an immersion blender. Prior to adding the veggies, strain the stock and place all the meat pieces on a separate plate. Add the veggies to the broth in the pot, bring to a boil, and simmer for 30 minutes. Once the vegetables are thoroughly cooked, puree with the immersion blender, then add the meat chunks back in. Heat the soup for 15 minutes more, add the olive oil and garlic paste, and serve.*

Ingredients:

1 pound beef stew meat

1 cinnamon stick

1 bay leaf

½ teaspoon ground white pepper

salt, to taste

6 cups water

2 large tomatoes, diced

4 carrots, peeled and sliced

2 medium zucchinis, tops sliced off and sliced

2 leeks, sliced *(with fibrous tips sliced off)*

3 medium onions, chopped

½ celery bunch, tips cut off and the stalks chopped

2 large potatoes, peeled and cut into chunks

1 cup chopped parsley

1 teaspoon cinnamon

½ teaspoon allspice

½ cup vermicelli, broken into small pieces

For serving:

⅓ cup olive oil

1 tablespoon garlic paste

Soups

Traditional Lentil Soup
(Adass Soup)

YIELD: 4 SERVINGS

Lentil soup is traditional for breaking the fast during the holy month of Ramadan, along with fattoush salad. It is absolutely satisfying, especially with fried croutons (kaak).

Directions:

Put the water and bouillon cube in a Dutch oven and add the lentils, potatoes, onions, carrots, salt, allspice, and cumin. Bring to a boil, lower the heat, and cover and simmer for 1 hour. Uncover if the soup is too watery.

Melt the butter in a medium-size skillet and fry the croutons until golden and crisp. Remove from the butter and set on paper towels to drain.

Puree the soup. Serve with the fried croutons.

Ingredients:

6 cups water

1 bouillon cube *(optional)*

1 cup red lentils

1 large baking potato, peeled and cut into chunks

2 large onions, chopped

2 carrots, peeled and sliced

Salt, to taste

1 teaspoon allspice

1 teaspoon cumin *(or more to taste)*

4 tablespoons clarified butter

2 cups pita croutons *(see Chapter 2, "Basics")*

CHAPTER 5

Mezzes: Dips, Finger Foods, Salads, and Sides

What is a traditional Lebanese mezze?

While the tradition of the mezze can be found throughout the Eastern Mediterranean region, it is generally admitted that the Lebanese have perfected the art of the mezze. In Lebanon, it is considered a national institution and a source of great pride.

What exactly is a mezze? In Lebanese culture, inviting someone to a mezze is an offer to casually taste various dishes presented in small plates while drinking a cocktail, preferably the country's anise-flavored drink of *arak*. A mezze can never take place in a time crunch!

The origin of the Lebanese mezze tradition is attributed to the town of Zahlé, located near a river, around the beginning of the twentieth century. At that time, there were only a couple of cafés near the riverbanks, and the mezze offered in these eateries was modest, consisting of a handful of small plates of roasted nuts with olives and fresh vegetables. Soon more cafés opened, and competition among the restaurateurs resulted in the mezze becoming more and more lavish, culminating in fifty or so dishes offered. Folks would meet at these restaurants for a mezze that would last several hours. The final hour would be reserved for smoking the water pipe (*argueeleh*), when the conversation would finally come to a standstill. This tradition became widespread and is now practiced all over the country, especially in cafés and restaurants alongside riverbanks or the seashore.

One can prepare a mezze at home when entertaining. A simple one might consist of plates of roasted nuts, pumpkin or watermelon seeds, olives, cucumbers, carrot sticks, savory pastries, white cheese balls in olive oil, fresh tomato slices, and radishes. A more elaborate mezze could include hummus,

fattoush salad, tabbouleh salad, fried eggplant and zucchini slices, kibbeh balls, and vegetables stewed in olive oil and onions.

The key to a good mezze is a convivial atmosphere—setting forth animated conversation or light banter leading to laughs and a good time. Serving arak at a mezze is strongly recommended; however, it is not mandatory. There are many wineries in the country that are producing fine wines exported throughout the world, and these could be offered at a mezze in addition to arak. Arak is a symbol of Lebanese mountain life. It is distilled from sweet grapes, is unsweetened, and flavored with anise. The drink itself is colorless, and when water is poured over it, it turns cloudy. It has a strong licorice taste and is about 45 percent alcohol.

Umm Elias (*Umm* is "mother" in Arabic, and her name indicates that she is the mother of Elias, her firstborn son) is a Lebanese farmer who lives in a village in the Chouf Mountains. I asked her once what her typical day was like, and this is what she said: "I spend all my day in the field, and I come home at night to have a bite to eat and drink my glass of arak; then I go to bed with a smile." She, of course, distills her own arak. Like many Lebanese mountain-dwellers, she reveres arak and views it as her comfort potion after a long day of toiling. (*Arak* is the word for "sweat" in Arabic.)

In this section, I have included dishes served at a mezze or as appetizers or side dishes during more formal meals. A mezze dish is always served on a small plate or in a small bowl next to other dishes of the same size. The traditional mezze vessels are made of glazed clay; however, any container will do as long as it is small.

Yogurt Cheese with Garlic Dip
(Labneh w-Toom)

YIELD: 4 SERVINGS

Taste of Beirut

This is a traditional mezze plate and just about the fastest one could put together. It is simply yogurt cheese mixed with a little garlic paste (to taste). The plate is garnished with fresh mint leaves and a drizzle of olive oil, and is served with pita bread or pita chips.

Ingredients:

1½ cups yogurt cheese
(2 batches; see Chapter 2, "Basics")

1 teaspoon garlic paste or 1 tablespoon garlic cream *(see Chapter 2, "Basics")*

¼ cup olive oil

2 sprigs fresh mint leaves, plucked from the stems

Pita bread

Directions:

Mix the garlic paste with the yogurt cheese in a bowl. Taste to adjust, adding more garlic paste, if desired. Transfer to a small mezze plate. With the back of a spoon, make a ridge all around the inside of the yogurt cheese. Drizzle olive oil to fill that ridge (more or less). Stick one or two mint sprigs in the middle of the plate. Serve with quartered pita bread or toasted pita chips.

Dips

Beet Dip *(Mama Dallou'ah)*

YIELD: 4 SERVINGS

Kameel Abu-Hatoum, a distinguished connoisseur of traditional Lebanese cuisine from Baakline (Chouf Mountains), graciously gave me the recipe for this dip. He coined it *mama dallou'ah*. This name was meant as a counter to the now world-famous baba ghanouj. *Baba* means "daddy" and *ghanouj* means "cuddly" (or someone who likes to spoil and cuddle their baby or loved one). *Mama* is "mom" and *dallou'ah* means a mom who loves to be pampered, cuddled, spoiled, and cherished. This is a delicious dip served at room temperature with pita bread. It is simple to prepare, and the taste can be adjusted a bit (more or less lemon, garlic, or tahini) according to taste. The tarator sauce can be prepared the day before *(see Chapter 2, "Basics")* and mixed with the beets later.

Ingredients:

1½ pounds beets

2 medium lemons, juiced *(about ⅓ to ½ cup juice)*

1 teaspoon garlic paste *(see Chapter 2, "Basics")*

½ cup tahini *(more to taste)*

1 tablespoon pomegranate molasses *(optional)*

¼ cup chopped Italian parsley

Directions:

1) Heat the oven to 375 degrees F. Wrap the beets in foil and roast them for 45 minutes or until tender. Peel and cut them into chunks and place them in the bowl of a food processor to cool for a few minutes.

2) Mix the tahini and ¼ cup of the lemon juice in a bowl and start stirring. As it curdles, add a bit of water. Add the garlic paste.

3) Set the processor in motion and gradually add the sauce to the beets through the feed tube, adding a touch of pomegranate molasses if desired; taste and adjust seasoning. Add more lemon juice if desired. Transfer to a serving platter. Garnish with the parsley and serve at room temperature with pita bread or chips.

NOTE: *The beets can be boiled whole in water for 30 minutes. Drain, peel, and proceed. To save time, use one cup of a ready-made tarator sauce (see Chapter 2, "Basics"). The amount of the sauce will vary slightly; the dip should be smooth but still a bit chunky with a good texture (not soupy), like a chickpea hummus.*

Dips

Swiss Chard Stalks Dip
(M'tabbal Dulu' el-Selek)

YIELD: 4 SERVINGS

This dip is made with the stalks of Swiss chard. It resembles the eggplant dip baba ghanouj in taste. It is composed of boiled chard stalks, tahini, garlic, and lemon juice. Traditionally, it was made when stuffed Swiss chard leaves were served. Instead of throwing away the stalks (which are too thick to roll anyway), they were recycled this way. The dip is presented beside the stuffed chard leaves and is served with pita bread. You may wish to pour a swirl of olive oil on the dip, which is also traditional. This dish is made with tarator sauce, which can be prepared ahead of time *(see Chapter 2, "Basics")*.

Ingredients:

3 cups of chopped Swiss chard stalks

1 tablespoon garlic paste *(see Chapter 2, "Basics")*

½ cup tahini

1 large lemon, juiced

¼ cup water

2 tablespoons olive oil, to garnish

Directions:

Place the stalks in a saucepan with one cup of water and bring to a boil. Gently boil (or steam) until tender. Drain and transfer to the bowl of a food processor and let it cool for a few minutes while you prepare the tarator sauce.

In a bowl, place the garlic paste, tahini, and lemon juice and stir to combine. Add the water and stir to make the sauce smoother.

Purée the chard stalks and combine them with the tarator sauce. Taste and adjust, adding more garlic paste, tahini, or lemon, as desired. Transfer to a serving dish and serve with pita bread.

Farmer plucking chard

NOTE: *This dish may also be prepared with yogurt instead of tahini.*

Red Lentil and Pumpkin Dip

YIELD: 4 SERVINGS

This dip came about by accident. I had lots of pumpkin from our orchard in the mountains, and we had eaten plenty of pumpkin kibbeh. I devised this dip hoping it would work. I was surprised and relieved when it met with everyone's approval. It did not last long!

Directions:

1) Heat the oil in a skillet and add the onions. Sauté over medium heat, adding the sugar after 12 minutes, and stir them from time to time until they caramelize.

2) Meanwhile, place the lentils in a saucepan with the water and bring to a simmer. Cook for 20 minutes.

3) Add the caramelized onions, pumpkin, pomegranate molasses, salt, cinnamon, paprika, and pepper to the saucepan. Cook the mixture for 15 minutes over very gentle heat, stirring from time to time and mashing the pumpkin with a meat mallet against the sides of the pan. Add the lemon juice. Keep an eye on the saucepan to make sure the mixture gets thicker but does not burn.

4) When most of the water has evaporated, turn off the heat and taste to adjust seasoning. Serve warm with corn chips or pita bread.

Ingredients:

⅓ cup oil

2 medium onions, chopped

1 teaspoon sugar

½ cup red lentils

3 cups water

1 pound pumpkin, peeled and cut up

1 tablespoon pomegranate molasses

1 teaspoon salt

½ teaspoon cinnamon

½ teaspoon paprika

½ teaspoon white pepper

1 medium lemon, juiced (*about 3 tablespoons*)

Corn chips or pita chips to serve

Dips

Classic Hummus *(Hummus M'tabbal)*

YIELD: 8 SERVINGS

Hummus is a fundamental part of a Lebanese mezze table and is served either plain or topped with meat and pine nuts. *Hummus* is the word for "chickpeas" in Arabic and also the name of the chickpea dip made with tahini. In Lebanese, the name of this dish, *hummus m'tabbal*, means "seasoned chickpeas," and it is an accurate title for this dish.

The goal is to achieve a balance of a very creamy yet firm texture, with an undercurrent of lemony and garlicky taste lingering on the palate after the hummus is gone.

Soak the chickpeas overnight with plenty of water. To save time, cook the chickpeas thoroughly and store them in freezer bags with a little chickpea water. This dip is made with tarator sauce *(see Chapter 2, "Basics")*, which can be prepared ahead.

Directions:

1) Drain the chickpeas and transfer them to a Dutch oven. Add the water and bring to a boil over medium heat, skimming the foam from the top. Lower the heat and simmer for about 2 hours.

2) Drain the chickpeas, reserving 1 cup of the cooking water in the pot. Set aside ¼ cup of the chickpeas for a garnish. Mash the remaining chickpeas in a food mill with the finest disc or in the bowl of a food processor.

3) Stir the tahini until the oil on the top is well incorporated, then add it, the lemon juice, and the garlic paste to the food mill (or food processor) and process until mixed. If the texture is too thick, add some of the cooking water. Taste and adjust, adding more tahini, lemon juice, or garlic, if desired.

Ingredients:

2 cups dry chickpeas, soaked in 8 cups of water overnight

8 cups water

1 teaspoon garlic paste *(see Chapter 2, "Basics")*

½ cup tahini *(more, to taste)*

3 medium lemons, freshly squeezed *(about ½ cup lemon juice)*

¼ cup extra-virgin olive oil, as garnish

1 teaspoon paprika or cumin as garnish

Pita bread, to serve

4) Pour the hummus into a bowl. Form a ridge all around within 2 inches of the border and pour the oil in it; sprinkle paprika or cumin on top. Garnish with the whole chickpeas and serve with fresh pita bread or pita chips.

Hummus can be made with canned chickpeas as well. Drain the cans and rinse the chickpeas, then transfer them to the bowl of a food processor. Proceed with the recipe, adjusting the amounts of garlic, lemon juice, and tahini to your taste. Add a bit of water if the paste is too thick.

NOTE: *A food mill set at the finest setting will give the smoothest hummus; it scrapes off the skins and is used by most old-fashioned cooks in Lebanon. If you find that your hummus is too runny, I learned this trick from my mother, who told me that restaurants in Beirut were doing it: Tear the crust of one or several slices of plain American white sandwich bread. Add the fresh bread to the processor to make bread crumbs and mix with the hummus. This will give it body and texture without taking away the taste. To save time, you can use prepared tarator sauce in this recipe instead of the garlic, tahini, and lemon juice (see Chapter 2, "Basics"). If you're using a food processor, drizzle it down the feed tube gradually, scraping the bowl and tasting every few minutes. Adjust to taste.*

Dips

Hummus with Meat
(Hummus Bel-Theeneh Bel-Laham)

YIELD: 4 SERVINGS

Ingredients:

2 tablespoons oil or clarified butter

½ pound ground meat *(lamb or beef)* or unflavored brisket *(cooked)*

1 teaspoon allspice

1 teaspoon salt, or to taste

½ teaspoon cinnamon

¼ cup toasted pine nuts *(see "Nuts" in Chapter 2, "Basics")*

1 batch classic hummus *(see recipe on p. 114)*

This is one of the most popular mezze items. When the meat and hummus plate arrives at the table, the meat sizzling and glistening with fat, it is hard to resist diving in and grabbing a mouthful with a piece of pita bread.

Directions:

Heat the oil in a medium-size skillet over medium heat. Add the meat, allspice, salt, and cinnamon. Separate the meat as it cooks to keep it in small bits. Sprinkle the pine nuts over the meat and toss a bit to combine. Place the meat and nuts in the middle of a plate of hummus and serve immediately.

NOTE: *Precooked chopped-up brisket can be a quick alternative, except it would need to be warmed up in the oil (with a drizzle of red wine vinegar) and sprinkled with the salt and spices. Add the pine nuts and serve on the hummus the same way.*

Dips

Red Pepper Hummus

YIELD: 4 SERVINGS

Ingredients:

1 cup roasted, peeled, and seeded red peppers

1 container *(15 ounces)* prepared hummus or 1 batch of classic hummus *(see recipe on p. 114)*

¼ cup lemon juice

¼ cup tahini *(to taste)*

1 teaspoon garlic paste *(or to taste)*

This recipe came about when I had roasted a few peppers and was at a loss as to what to do with them. I was making a classic hummus, the chickpeas were getting pureed in the food processor, and I just threw all my peppers in there, hoping that the resulting concoction would be edible. This red pepper hummus won approval across the board and the supply was consumed quickly.

Directions:

Put all of the ingredients into the bowl of a food processor and puree. Taste to adjust, adding more lemon juice, tahini, or garlic paste, if desired. Serve with pita bread or raw veggie sticks.

NOTE: *To save time, jarred piquillo peppers or red peppers can be used.*

Dips

Chickpea and Potato Ball (Topig)

YIELD: 8 SERVINGS

There is a large Armenian community established in Lebanon. The Armenians are fully integrated into Lebanese society, and even participate in the government with deputies, ministers, and political parties. However, they have remained steadfastly faithful to their culture and heritage. One of my aunts who visited Armenia came back with tales of a beautiful country with pristine lakes, majestic mountains, ancient monasteries, and captivating archaeological sites.

This is an Armenian specialty called *topig*, which means "little ball." It is eaten as an appetizer during Lent, which for the Armenian Orthodox is a lengthy affair, extending forty days. It is vegan and is composed of chickpeas, onions, tahini, and spices. It would make a conversation starter at a dinner party, as it is not a dish many people have had before.

Taste of Beirut

Directions:

For the shell:

Place the chickpeas and potato in a food mill (or food processor), along with the tahini, turmeric, pepper, and salt. Mix until mashed and doughy. Set aside.

For the filling:

Heat the oil in a large skillet over medium heat. Sauté the onions until caramelized. Add the pecans, currants, cumin, cinnamon, allspice, 1 teaspoon of the salt, and the cloves. Add just enough tahini to make a moist filling.

To make the balls:

1) Divide the chickpea and potato dough into 4 equal balls. Place each ball in the middle of a large piece of plastic wrap or foil. Roll it out gently into a 9-inch circle. Place one quarter of the filling in the middle of the circle. Enclose the filling with the dough, using the plastic wrap or foil to do so (lifting it up from underneath). Tie each filled ball securely with a piece of kitchen string. Repeat with the remaining balls. Place in the fridge for a few hours or overnight.

2) Serve the balls at room temperature; sprinkle them with paprika (or cinnamon) and drizzle lemon juice and olive oil on them. Include lemon quarters on the plate, and serve with a decanter of olive oil and pita chips or water crackers.

Ingredients:

For the shell:

2 cans *(15.5 ounces each)* chickpeas, rinsed and drained

1 large baking potato, cooked and peeled

¼ cup tahini

1 teaspoon turmeric

½ teaspoon white pepper

Salt, to taste

For the filling:

½ cup extra-virgin olive oil

2 pounds onions, sliced

¼ cup toasted pecans *(or almonds, walnuts, or pine nuts; see "Nuts" in Chapter 2, "Basics")*

¼ cup currants *(or raisins or dried cranberries)*

1 teaspoon cumin

1 teaspoon cinnamon *(more, if used for garnish)*

1 teaspoon allspice

2 teaspoons salt

½ teaspoon ground cloves

½ cup tahini *(more or less as needed)*

To serve:

¼ cup fresh lemon juice

Paprika or cinnamon

1 lemon, sliced thinly

Olive oil

Pita chips or water crackers

Eggplant Dip *(Baba Ghanouj)*

YIELD: 4 SERVINGS

Eggplant is one of those vegetables I hated as a kid but love as an adult. Lebanese cuisine has dozens of outstanding eggplant dishes. This one is by far the easiest to prepare and the most popular. It is served at every mezze.

To be delicious, this dish needs to be light (almost ethereal) with a faint lemony/garlicky subterranean flavor. When I complimented my dear aunt Wadad on her baba ghanouj, she replied that she barely adds any tahini, so as to avoid ruining it. I could have swallowed the entire platter, but I didn't out of consideration for the other guests at her table.

Ingredients:

1½ pounds large, shiny, and smooth eggplant

2 teaspoons garlic paste *(see Chapter 2, "Basics")*

1 medium lemon, juiced *(about 3 tablespoons juice)*

1 tablespoon pomegranate molasses *(optional)*

¼ cup tahini

Pomegranate arils, for garnish

Directions:

If you have a gas grill or stove, place the eggplant on the burner and let it darken and blister, turning it to make sure it gets blackened all over. Transfer the eggplant to a colander set over a bowl to cool. Once cool, peel them and mash them a bit. Drain for 30 minutes. Transfer to a mixer or food processor bowl and add the rest of the ingredients, tasting to adjust. Sprinkle with pomegranate arils if desired, and a trickle of olive oil.

NOTE: *The smoky flavor of the eggplants obtained by charring them over the open flame is essential to a good baba ghanouj. If this is not possible, canned baba ghanouj can be used instead. Doctored up with lemon juice, garlic paste, and tahini, it is a passable substitute.*

Dips

Red Pepper and Walnut Dip
(Muhammara)

YIELD: 12 OUNCES

This dip originated in Aleppo, Syria, and was meant to accompany meats. The original version uses lots of walnuts flavored with cumin, pomegranate molasses, and a tad of red pepper paste. Here, I switched it around by using a larger amount of red bell peppers and using the walnuts as an accent instead of the main ingredient. It turned out to be a very versatile dip, and I have since used it to make quick pasta or seafood sauces, to slather on rolls or flatbreads, or to add a quick burst of flavor to dressings or marinades. You can freeze it in small bags for extra convenience.

Ingredients:

3 large red bell peppers

1 small onion, quartered

1 tablespoon garlic paste *(see Chapter 2, "Basics")*, or to taste

½ cup walnuts, previously soaked for one hour and drained

½ cup plain bread crumbs

1 teaspoon ground cumin

1 tablespoon pomegranate molasses

1 teaspoon red chili paste *(or Aleppo pepper or smoked paprika)*

1 teaspoon salt

⅓ cup olive oil, more if needed *(if the dip is too dry)*

Directions:

1) Wash the peppers and place them on a foil-lined cookie sheet under the broiler 4 or 5 inches from the heat source, turning them every few minutes until the skin is blackened and charred.

2) Place the peppers in a plastic bag with a couple of tablespoons of water and close the bag tightly for 10 minutes. Open the bag and peel off the skins of the peppers. Cut the peppers open and discard all the seeds and white parts inside, as well as the stem.

3) Place the peppers, onion, garlic, walnuts, bread crumbs, cumin, pomegranate molasses, red chili paste or paprika, salt, and oil in the bowl of a food processor. Process for 1 minute or until the mixture is smooth yet still thick and with some texture. Taste to adjust seasoning and transfer the sauce to a bowl. Cover and refrigerate.

NOTE: *This recipe can be made with jarred roasted peppers, such as piquillo peppers, to save time. The traditional recipe doubles up the amount of walnuts. In Syria it is often prepared by using red pepper paste (without using any bell peppers) and a few tablespoons of tahini.*

Dips

Avocado with Yogurt Cheese and Tomato Dip

YIELD: 1½ CUPS

Ingredients:

2 large avocados

¼ cup yogurt cheese
(see Chapter 2, "Basics")

1 large tomato, diced small

1 small white onion,
chopped fine

Salt, to taste

1 tablespoon lemon juice

1 tablespoon sumac,
to garnish

Directions:

Halve the avocados,
remove the pits, and scoop
the flesh into a bowl and
mash. Add the rest of the
ingredients, except the
sumac, and mix well. If you
like, scoop the dip back into
the empty avocado shells,
garnish with a sprinkling
of the sumac, and serve
with pita chips.

Dips

Chicken Bites with Dukkah

YIELD: 4 SERVINGS

This dish consists of ground chicken combined with spices and coated in a traditional Egyptian concoction called *dukkah*. Dukkah comes from the root verb *duk* "to knock" or "to pound" in Arabic. In other words, the mixture of nuts and spices are pounded. The origin of dukkah was explained to me by Salah, an Egyptian farmer who moved to Lebanon for work. Years ago, salt was only available in Egypt in blocks (from the Mediterranean). Therefore, each home had a large and heavy mortar in solid brass called a *hone* (the mallet alone weighed 6 pounds), which was used to grind salt. Spices were added to create dukkah. Salah told me that whenever a woman was married off, she'd be given her own hone to grind her salt and dukkah (each family in Egypt has a personal dukkah mix). This mortar is found in Levantine and Kurdish traditions as well, with the same name, which tells me that it is a shared tradition throughout the Middle East. One friend, Hoda Sweid, whose mother grew up in Egypt, even showed me her mom's hone, brought back with her to Lebanon after she left Egypt permanently.

Directions:

1) Mix the chicken with the onion, 1 tablespoon of the lemon juice, and the egg yolk, sumac, pepper, paprika, cinnamon, and salt. Set aside.

2) Put the flour into a bowl. Put the whole eggs into another bowl and beat slightly. Put the dukkah in a third bowl.

3) Shape the chicken mixture into balls about the size of walnuts. Dip the balls in the flour, then in the egg, then in the dukkah.

4) Heat the oil over medium heat in a large and deep skillet. Drop the chicken pieces into the oil and cook for about 5 minutes, front and back. When the pieces feel firm and look toasted, remove them and set them on a platter lined with paper towels to drain.

5) Peel, pit, and mash the avocados in a bowl with the yogurt or yogurt cheese and garlic paste. Taste and adjust.

6) Arrange the chicken bites on a plate and serve with sliced tomatoes and avocados in pita bread, or serve as an appetizer with a bowl of avocado dressing.

Ingredients:

1 pound ground chicken breasts

1 small onion, chopped fine

1 tablespoon plus 2 teaspoons fresh lemon juice

1 egg yolk, plus 2 whole eggs

1 teaspoon sumac

½ teaspoon white pepper

½ teaspoon paprika

½ teaspoon cinnamon

Salt, to taste

2 cups flour

1 bag dukkah *(approximately 1 cup) (or make your own mix; see recipe following this one)*

4 cups vegetable oil *(for frying)*

2 ripe avocados

¼ cup plain yogurt or 3 tablespoons yogurt cheese *(see Chapter 2, "Basics")*

½ teaspoon garlic paste *(see Chapter 2, "Basics")*

Pita bread

Dukkah Spice Mix

YIELD: 2 CUPS

The only constant spices used for dukkah are cumin, coriander, salt, black pepper, and chili pepper. This recipe can be altered based on your taste. You can use dukkah in many different ways: as a dip (mix in a small bowl with olive oil) for pita bread or fresh veggies, as a condiment for grilled meats, or as a topping for breadsticks. I enlisted my Egyptian friend Phoebe to help me devise this dukkah.

Ingredients:

½ cup almonds, chopped

½ cup pecans, chopped (or pistachios or other nuts)

1½ cups sesame seeds

½ cup whole coriander seeds

1 tablespoon cumin

½ cup ground coriander

1 teaspoon salt

½ teaspoon black pepper

1 teaspoon chili powder (optional)

Directions:

1) In a large skillet set on medium heat, toast the almonds and pecans until fragrant, about 8–10 minutes. Remove them from the skillet and put them on a baking sheet to cool. In the same skillet, toast the sesame seeds until light golden brown, stirring occasionally so they don't burn (about 8–10 minutes). Pour them into a bowl immediately to cool. Toast the whole coriander seeds in the same skillet until they begin to pop. Remove them from the heat and cool.

2) Crush the cooled nuts in a coffee grinder and pour the mix into a bowl. Crush the sesame seeds and whole coriander seeds as well and transfer them to the bowl with the nuts.

3) Add the cumin, ground coriander, salt, pepper, and chili powder, if using. Mix well. Store whatever you are not using right away in the freezer.

Finger foods

Olives in a Spiced Tomato Sauce
(Salatet Zaytoon)

YIELD: 8 SERVINGS

Olives and olive oil are the pillars of Lebanese food and traditions, and they have been an intrinsic part of the Lebanese diet for centuries. Olives are called "poor man's meat" *(al-zaytoon laham al-fakeer)*. Not only are olives harvested and brined every year but their oil is used both in cooking and as a condiment for most dishes. In fact, in the villages, folks use olive oil to make soap. It was not until the sixties that olive oil's primary use for cooking took a backseat and was replaced by soya and corn oil, which flooded the local Lebanese market with an aggressive price structure. Prior to that time, olive oil was always used for cooking. Nevertheless, a Lebanese table at home or in any restaurant would not be complete without a plate of olives with which to start and finish a meal. Olives also figure at a breakfast table with bread, olives are nibbled on at lunch before the main dish, and olives are savored with some cheese and bread for a light dinner. This explains why olives have been called "sheikh of the table" in a proverbial expression.

This is my attempt to recreate an olive salad I tasted in a restaurant in the town of Barouk in the Chouf Mountains. It was served as part of a mezze, and I loved the idea of combining stewed tomatoes with olives. Break a bite-size piece of pita bread to scoop up the olives and sauce.

Ingredients:

¼ cup olive oil

3 scallions, chopped

4 medium ripe tomatoes, diced

2 tablespoons red pepper paste *(mild or hot)*

½ teaspoon ground coriander

¼ teaspoon black pepper

2 cups green olives

¼ cup chopped Italian parsley

Directions:

Heat the oil in a skillet over medium-low heat and sauté the scallions for about 5 minutes. Add the tomatoes, red pepper paste, coriander, and pepper. Stir and cover the skillet for 15 minutes. Turn off the heat, uncover the skillet, add the olives, taste to adjust seasoning, and cool. Transfer to a serving plate garnished with chopped parsley. Serve with a basket of pita bread.

NOTE: *The red pepper paste can be replaced with a dash of chili powder or smoked paprika.*

Finger foods

Zucchini Fritters

YIELD: 4 SERVINGS

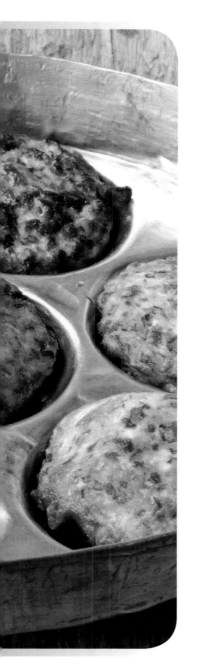

4 large eggs

2 cups grated zucchini or
zucchini pulp

1 cup chopped parsley
(or mixture of herbs)

1 small white onion, chopped

1 teaspoon garlic paste
(see Chapter 2, "Basics")

½ teaspoon salt

¼ teaspoon pepper

1 cup olive oil

This is a great way to use leftover zucchini. In Lebanon, these fritters are made with the zucchini pulp that is left over after they have been cored for stuffing. Simply grate or shred the zucchini in a food processor, add a bit of grated onion, garlic paste, and lots of chopped herbs, and sauté them in olive oil for a few minutes on each side.

Directions:

In a large bowl, beat the eggs and add the zucchini, parsley, onion, and garlic. Season with salt and pepper to taste. Heat the oil in a large skillet and drop small (about ¼ cup) ladles of the mixture in the hot oil. Fry on both sides and serve warm or at room temperature.

VARIATION: Another method consists of stir-frying the shredded zucchini first in a skillet with 3 tablespoons of oil and garlic. The onions can also be sautéed previously and added to the mixture. This step intensifies the flavor of both the zucchini and the onions.

Finger foods

Spinach Turnovers
(Fatayer Bel-Sabanegh)

YIELD: 35 SMALL TURNOVERS

These spinach turnovers are in the top three best savory pastries on the Lebanese table. Not only are they light and vegan, they can be made with other greens as well. In Lebanon, mountain residents like to fill them with wild sorrel *(hummaydah)* or purslane *(bakleh)*. The pastries freeze very well, for about two weeks.

Taste of Beirut

Directions:

1) Cut the dough into 6 small balls. Sprinkle flour on a large tray and set each ball of dough on the tray, dousing it lightly with the flour. Cover with a cloth and turn your attention to the stuffing.

2) Chop the spinach coarsely with the stems. Place the spinach and onions in a large colander and sprinkle with the remaining sumac, salt, and pepper. Set over the sink and squeeze the moisture from the mix. Transfer the mix to a large bowl.

3) Mix the oil and lemon juice in a small bowl. Pour the dressing over the spinach mix until it is moistened but no more than that. If the mix is too wet, it causes the turnovers to open up.

4) Preheat the oven to 375 degrees F. Roll out the dough on a floured counter, one ball at a time, as thin as possible. Cut out rounds with a cookie cutter (or the rim of a glass). Place 1 tablespoon of stuffing on each turnover. Lift the turnover on two sides and pinch them first to enclose the circle. Lift the remaining side and pinch to seal to the other two sides to form a pyramid. Place the pyramids on greased cookie sheets. Brush the tops with olive oil. Bake 15 minutes or until the tops and bottoms are golden. Serve at room temperature.

Ingredients:

One batch dough
  (see Chapter 2, "Basics")
  made without yeast

2 pounds fresh spinach,
  washed and sprinkled
  with salt and half the
  sumac

4 large onions, chopped fine

¼ cup ground sumac

1 tablespoon salt, plus more
  as needed

1 teaspoon black pepper
  (or white pepper)

⅓ cup extra-virgin olive oil,
  plus more to brush on
  the turnovers

¼ cup lemon juice

⅓ cup pine nuts, soaked in
  a bowl of water for one
  hour (optional)

Finger foods

mini meat Pies (Sfeeha)

YIELD: MAKES 40 SFEEHAS

If there is one pastry item from the Lebanese kitchen deserving of a standing ovation, it is *sfeeha* (pronounced s-fee-ha with the "a" like "apple"). What is sfeeha? A mini meat pie, made extraordinary by the folks in Baalbek (the number one tourist destination in Lebanon, site of thousand-year-old Roman temples and an annual performing arts festival). A few well-known butcher shops prepare it onsite. Folks will tell you that it is the lamb fat that makes these so good. Whatever the reason, they are irresistible, especially when prepared to order by a specialist. At home, though, your own personal concoction of spices and add-ons can be developed to please family and friends. Its shape can be just like a cocktail-size pie or pinched on all four sides. The key is that the meat filling has to cook with the dough, exuding a fragrance that permeates the kitchen. If you make these for a party, bake them when your guests arrive.

My grandmother's version was very plain and only added onion and a bit of yogurt cheese to the meat paste. I prefer mine with tomato and red pepper paste, pomegranate molasses, tahini, and a bit of yogurt cheese. Apparently, so did my son and his buddy. I made a batch once that I left on the kitchen counter, and it did not take long before they were devoured.

Directions:

1) Let the dough rise for 1 hour or longer. In a large bowl, mix the meat, salt, allspice, cinnamon, Aleppo pepper or cayenne, red pepper paste, tomato paste, parsley, pomegranate molasses, tahini, yogurt cheese, garlic paste, and pepper.

2) Squeeze and drain the onion and add it to the meat mixture. Mix well. Cover the mix and put it in the fridge.

3) Heat the oven to 375 degrees F. Line two cookie sheets with parchment paper.

4) Transfer the dough to a floured work surface and punch it to remove all the air pockets. Roll it into a large circle, about ⅛ inch thick, then cut out rounds with a 3-inch cookie cutter.

5) Remove the meat mix from the refrigerator and stir it a few times. Place a tablespoon of the filling in the center of each dough circle. Pinch opposite ends of the circle together, bringing up the edges of the dough. This will enclose the meat filling, forming a square with higher edges, and will prevent the filling from slipping out during baking.

6) Using a spatula to lift them up, place the pies on the baking sheets. Sprinkle them with pine nuts or almonds, pressing them into the dough or meat mixture to make sure they adhere. Bake for 10 minutes or until the pies are golden. Serve with a bowl of yogurt and lemon quarters on the side.

Ingredients:

1 batch dough
(see Chapter 2, "Basics")

Filling:

¾ pound ground lamb *(or beef)*

1½ teaspoons sea salt

½ teaspoon allspice

½ teaspoon cinnamon

½ teaspoon red Aleppo pepper or cayenne pepper *(or smoked paprika)*

1 tablespoon red pepper paste *(optional)*

2 tablespoons tomato paste *(or 4 diced tomatoes)*

½ cup (packed) chopped Italian parsley

2 tablespoons pomegranate molasses

3 tablespoons tahini

3 tablespoons yogurt cheese, or yogurt drained for 4 hours *(see Chapter 2, "Basics")*

½ teaspoon garlic paste

¼ teaspoon black pepper

1 large onion, chopped fine

¼ cup shortening *(or clarified butter or oil)*

¼ cup toasted pine nuts or sliced almonds *(see "Nuts" in Chapter 2, "Basics")*

2 cups yogurt

2 lemons, quartered

Finger foods

Pumpkin Fries

YIELD: 4 SERVINGS

Ingredients:

1 pound pumpkin

1 tablespoon sumac

¼ cup water

1 teaspoon salt

3 cups oil

One of many side dishes in Lebanese cuisine consists of large slices of pumpkin panfried and served with a garlic and lemon dressing. I thought it would be more fun to cut the pumpkin like french fries and dress them with sumac. Sumac dressing is common, especially in mountain villages where sumac grows in every corner.

Directions:

1) Peel the pumpkin and cut into 3-inch-long sticks, like thick french fries.

2) Place the sumac in a small bowl and add the water and salt. Stir to dissolve the salt. After about a half hour, strain the sumac water into a bowl.

3) Heat the oil over medium-high heat in a large skillet. Fry the pumpkin fries for about 6 minutes or until golden. Drain on paper towels.

4) Empty the skillet of all the oil and transfer the pumpkin fries back into the skillet. Pour the strained sumac water over the fries and cook a few minutes longer so the fries soak up the juice. Serve.

NOTE: *This dish would be fun to eat with a side of garlic cream* (see Chapter 2, "Basics" for recipe).

Finger foods

Cheese Rolls *(Fatayer Be-Jeben)*

YIELD: MAKES 35 ROLLS

These cheese and herb rolls are a fixture at any gathering. They can be prepared in advance, frozen, and heated on the spot.

Ingredients:

One batch dough
 (see Chapter 2, "Basics")

1 cup finely chopped
 white onion

½ teaspoon salt

12 ounces shredded white
 cheese (mozzarella,
 Monterey Jack, or akkawi)

8 ounces feta

1 cup minced parsley

1 teaspoon allspice

2 large egg whites

1 large egg yolk

1 tablespoon water or milk

Directions:

1) Let the dough rise while you prepare the cheese stuffing, about 1 hour (or longer).

2) Put the onions in a sieve over the top of a bowl, sprinkle with salt, and let them drip their juice for at least 30 minutes. Squeeze any remaining juice from the onions.

3) In a bowl, combine the onions, cheese, feta, parsley, allspice, and egg whites. Mix well to combine.

4) Once the dough has risen, punch it down and transfer it to a floured work surface. Roll it into a large circle. Cut rounds with a cookie cutter or the rim of a glass. Place a tablespoon of cheese filling on each round and pinch the ends to form little rolls.

5) Whisk the egg yolk with the water or milk. Brush the tops of the rolls for a shiny crust, if desired.

6) Place the rolls on a cookie sheet lined with parchment paper. Let them sit for 30 minutes.

7) Heat the oven to 375 degrees F. Bake for 10 minutes or until the rolls are golden and puffed up. Serve immediately.

NOTE: *To save time, skip the step on draining the juice from the onions. If you are planning to freeze these, omit adding onions.*

Finger foods

Swiss Chard Leaves with Rice and Herbs (Warak Selek Mehshi Bel-Zeit)

YIELD: 4 SERVINGS

Grape leaves are not the only leaves that get stuffed in Lebanon. Swiss chard leaves get stuffed as well, especially when it is no longer grape leaf season. If I do not have access to fresh grape leaves, Swiss chard leaves are my next choice. Upon simmering slowly and cooling, Swiss chard leaves develop an irresistible melt-in-the-mouth texture.

The general direction when preparing the stuffing for Swiss chard leaves (as well as grape leaves) was given to me by Asma, a seasoned chef in Beirut. It consists of preparing the stuffing as if making tabbouleh, except the bulgur is replaced with rice. In other words, the stuffing will have lots of chopped parsley, tomatoes, and onion but a *small* amount of rice.

Directions:

1) Put the parsley, mint, chopped onions, and diced tomatoes in a large bowl. Sprinkle salt, pepper, and allspice onto the mixture. Add ½ cup of the lemon juice and ½ cup of the oil, as well as the rice and the reserved juices from the tomatoes. Mix well and set aside. Sprinkle the sugar on the mixture and combine.

2) Fill a large pot with water and bring to a boil. Wash the chard and remove the stalks from the leaves (you can recycle the stalks by using them in the Swiss Chard Stalks Dip on p. 110). Cut the leaves into rectangles or squares, drop them into the pot, and blanch for mere seconds until limp. Remove immediately and drain in a colander.

3) Line a Dutch oven with the sliced onions, tomatoes, and potatoes. Place an elongated tablespoon of stuffing at the edge of the wide end of the leaf and roll it up like a cigar. Repeat the process with the remaining leaves. Remember not to roll them too tightly, as the rice will expand during cooking. Place the stuffed leaves seam side down in the pot. Place a plate on top in order to hold the leaves in place. Asma also places a 4-inch-wide rock (found at the beach) on top of the plate for extra protection.

4) Pour the remaining lemon juice, oil, any remaining juices from the stuffing, and a small cup of water over the leaves. The leaves need to be almost covered by the liquid. Cover the pot and simmer gently on medium-low heat for 45 minutes to 1 hour. Cool in the pot. When ready to serve, remove the plate and flip the pot onto a deep serving platter.

NOTE: *This dish can be prepared with grape leaves when they're in season.*

Ingredients:

3 bunches Italian parsley, chopped

1 bunch mint, chopped

4 small white onions *(2 chopped and 2 cut in slices)*

5 tomatoes *(3 diced small and 2 sliced; reserve juice in a bowl)*

1½ teaspoon salt

½ teaspoon black pepper

1 teaspoon allspice

¾ cup lemon juice

¾ cup olive oil

¾ cup rice *(preferably medium-grain starchy rice, such as sushi, Egyptian, Turkish, or Italian)*

1 teaspoon sugar

1 pound Swiss chard leaves

2 medium to large potatoes, sliced

Finger foods

Stuffed Mushrooms with Roasted Green Wheat

YIELD: 8 SERVINGS

Roasted green wheat, aka freekeh, is smoked wheat berries. It is available at all Arab groceries and online. It is prepared like rice, then coated in fat, boiled in a liquid, and served. There are two types of freekeh: one in which the berries are whole and the other in which they are broken up. The whole freekeh will require more time to cook, and more water. I devised this dish as a way to use up some leftover freekeh. The lamb confit can be replaced with bacon, chicken, or duck fat. It gives another layer of rustic flavor to the dish.

Directions:

1) Clean the mushrooms and remove the stems, reserving the caps whole. Finely chop the mushroom stems.

2) Melt the lamb confit (or bacon or chicken fat) in a saucepan over medium heat and sauté the onion. When translucent, add the mushroom stems and sauté until soft. Add the pepper, garlic paste, salt (cautiously as the lamb confit or bacon are already salted), and freekeh, and stir for 2 minutes until the grains are coated in fat.

3) Add the water or bouillon to the saucepan. Cover and simmer the mixture for 25 minutes or longer, until the freekeh is cooked and soft and silky. If necessary, add more water. (The amount of water and the cooking time depends on whether the freekeh is whole or broken up; the whole kernels may require more water to cook thoroughly.)

4) Heat the oven to 350 degrees F. While the freekeh is cooking, place the mushroom caps on a baking sheet covered in aluminum foil. Drizzle the oil on the caps and roast until browned and softened (about 8–10 minutes). Remove from the oven.

5) When the freekeh is fully cooked, fill the mushroom caps with the mixture. Before serving, heat the mushrooms for 5 minutes in a 300-degree F oven and sprinkle with the chopped parsley right before serving.

Ingredients:

1 pound white button mushrooms

2 or 3 tablespoons lamb confit (awarma), or bacon or chicken fat

1 small onion, chopped

½ teaspoon black pepper

1 teaspoon garlic paste

Salt, to taste

½ cup roasted green wheat (freekeh) (see p. 10)

1 cup water or bouillon (or use a bouillon cube with the water)

½ cup olive oil

¼ cup chopped parsley

Finger foods

Fattoush Salad

YIELD: 8 SERVINGS

NOTE: *Fry the pita croutons in the morning and keep them in a tightly closed container. They will keep for days.*

As essential to a Lebanese mezze table as the eternal hummus, this salad also signals the beginning of warm weather, lazy days at the beach, or hikes in the mountains. It is also served during the holy month of Ramadan with lentil soup. Some essential features of a good fattoush include crisp pita croutons, preferably fried; a copious amount of sumac dressing; fresh garden vegetables and herbs, such as tomatoes, cucumbers, radishes, green peppers, parsley, and mint; and last, but not least, purslane.

Purslane (Portulaca oleracea) is a leafy green found in North and South America, as well as in Europe, Asia, and all over the Middle East. It is very popular in Lebanon, where it is one of the main components of fattoush salad and used in lieu of spinach in many dishes, dumplings, and turnovers.

According to experts, it is among the most nutritious vegetables, with high amounts of omega-3s, calcium, iron, and vitamin A. I found it in the Middle Eastern grocery in Dallas, as well as at the Latino markets, where it is named verdolaga (bakleh in Arabic).

Directions:

Whisk the salad dressing ingredients in a salad bowl. Add the salad ingredients and toss to combine. Top the salad with the croutons and toss quickly to mix. Serve immediately.

Ingredients:

For the salad dressing:

2 medium lemons, juiced (about ⅓ to ½ cup juice)

¾ cup extra-virgin olive oil

¼ cup sumac (soaked in the lemon juice)

1 teaspoon garlic paste (see Chapter 2, "Basics")

Salt, to taste

For the salad:

1 head romaine or butter lettuce, torn in pieces

1 bunch purslane, leaves only

6 cucumbers (Armenian, Persian, English hothouse, or pickling cucumbers), sliced (about 3 cups)

6 medium to large tomatoes, diced

1 bunch radishes, sliced (use the leaves for this salad or another salad)

1 bunch green onions, sliced

1 cup chopped Italian parsley

½ cup chopped mint leaves

1 green bell pepper, diced

To serve:

4 cups fried croutons (see Chapter 2, "Basics")

Dandelion Greens Salad
(Salatet al-Hindbeh)

YIELD: 4 SERVINGS

If your partner is a carnivore, and after asking you, "What is for dinner?" the answer is "Dandelion salad with cheese," you will likely hear grumbling or protests. But this salad is served with a heap of fried onion rings. The dandelions are coated with olive oil, making them taste rich and mellow. The salad is served at room temperature. It is one of the most popular salads for mezzes across Lebanon. It is served at light dinners in homes everywhere as well.

I have met folks in the Lebanese mountains who make this salad with wild dandelions foraged that day. I go to the supermarket and get the organic ones if possible. Dandelions are loaded with iron, calcium, and antioxidants; with a side of fried *halloumi* cheese slices, this is a complete meal. (Halloumi is a semi-hard, brined cheese made from goat's milk or sheep's milk that is originally from Cyprus and very popular in Lebanon; it is sold at all Middle Eastern stores.)

Ingredients:

2 bunches dandelions

¾ cup olive oil

4 large onions, sliced

1 tablespoon garlic paste *(see Chapter 2, "Basics")*

Salt, to taste

¼ teaspoon ground black pepper, to taste

¼ cup fried pine nuts or sliced almonds

2 medium lemons, quartered

Directions:

1) Wash the dandelions well and cut off the tough ends. Boil a few cups of salted water in a pot and drop the dandelions in for a couple of minutes, then dunk them in an ice-water bowl. Remove immediately and squeeze them dry. Set them aside on a cutting board.

2) Heat the oil in a large skillet over medium heat and fry the onion rings until they caramelize. Transfer half the onions to a plate.

3) Chop the dandelions coarsely. Drop them in the skillet and fry them in the remaining oil. Add the garlic paste and salt and pepper (to taste), and stir to combine evenly into the greens.

4) Remove the greens from the skillet and place them on a platter, top with the rest of the onions, and garnish with the pine nuts or almonds; serve with extra lemon quarters.

NOTE: *After slicing the onions, you can sprinkle them with salt to make them purge their juices so they will fry to a crispier state. The pine nuts or almonds can be fried in a dab of butter until caramel-colored before using as a garnish. The dandelions can be prepared earlier in the day and fried in olive oil and garlic right before serving.*

Salads and Sides

Bulgur Salad in Eggplant Boats
(Labaniyet al-Burghul)

YIELD: UP TO 8 SERVINGS AS AN APPETIZER OR 4 SERVINGS AS A MAIN DISH

No wonder the eggplant has been crowned the sheikh of all vegetables in the Middle East. You will be reminded of that title once you taste it in this dish — resplendent in its silky smoothness, its belly bursting with a creamy, tangy, and rustic interior; fine bulgur soaked in pomegranate-scented juice; labneh (yogurt cheese) sparkling from a touch of garlic; and an array of fresh herbs and spices for that garden-fresh taste. It's a perfect dish for a buffet party to enjoy at room temperature.

Directions:

1) Line a sieve with a coffee filter or cheese-cloth and place it over a bowl. Place the yogurt in the sieve and drain it for 4 hours before making the salad.

2) Peel the eggplants, keeping the caps on, and sprinkle with salt. Place them in a colander and let them sweat for 30 minutes or longer.

3) Put the bulgur in a bowl. Dilute the pome-granate molasses in the hot water and pour over the bulgur; set aside.

4) Wipe the eggplants dry and heat the oil in a large skillet on medium heat. Fry the eggplants on all sides until browned and soft. Remove from the skillet and place on a plate lined with paper towels to soak up the excess oil. Set on a serving plate.

5) Place the drained yogurt in the salad bowl with the bulgur. Add the garlic paste, parsley, mint, dill, and basil, as well as the hot pepper, sun-dried tomatoes, and scallions. If the salad is too stiff, add some undrained yogurt to the mix. Taste and adjust seasonings.

6) With a small, sharp knife, make a slit alongside the length of the eggplants. Open up the eggplants gently with a spoon and fill the cavities with the bulgur and yogurt salad. Garnish with the pine nuts and serve at room temperature with pita bread.

Ingredients:

12 ounces plain yogurt, drained 4 hours or so

2 pounds baby eggplants

1 teaspoon salt

½ cup fine bulgur *(#1)*

1½ tablespoons pomegranate molasses

½ cup hot water

½ cup olive oil *(more as needed)*

1 tablespoon garlic paste *(see Chapter 2, "Basics")*

½ cup chopped Italian parsley

½ cup of assorted fresh mint, fresh dill, and fresh basil

½ teaspoon hot Aleppo pepper or smoked chili powder *(optional)*

2 tablespoons chopped sun-dried tomatoes *(optional)*

½ cup finely chopped scallions

¼ cup toasted pine nuts *(see "Nuts" in Chapter 2, "Basics")*

Pita bread, to serve

NOTE: *If you cannot locate baby eggplants (they can be found in Middle Eastern, Asian, or Indian grocery stores), serve this salad in a bowl or cupped in a cabbage leaf or romaine lettuce leaves.*

Salads and Sides

Yogurt and Cucumber Salad
(Salatet al-Laban w-Khyar)

YIELD: 4 TO 8 SERVINGS

This yogurt salad is a mainstay of the Lebanese table. It is always served with kibbeh pies, stuffed leaves and veggies (when stuffed with meat and rice), rice or bulgur pilafs, and kebabs. It is light and refreshing, easy to prepare, and very healthful. Lebanese cucumbers are very small, almost seedless, and very crunchy. The American pickling cucumbers or the English hothouse ones would make a good substitute. Lebanese cucumbers are found in some Middle Eastern stores, as well as another seedless variety of cucumbers sold under the name of Armenian or Persian cucumbers.

A similar salad is prepared in rural areas with purslane instead of cucumbers *(Ayran w Ba'kleh)*. Another version of this yogurt salad can be made with Swiss chard stalks, cut into small sticks, and boiled briefly first. Personally, I like to use fresh celery stalks (diced in tiny bits), as it keeps its crunch far longer than cucumber.

Ingredients:

16 ounces plain organic yogurt

4 cucumbers, peeled and diced

1 tablespoon garlic paste *(see Chapter 2, "Basics")*

1 tablespoon dried mint powder

Salt, to taste

1 fresh mint sprig, to garnish

Directions:

Pour the yogurt into a bowl. Beat it for a few seconds with a wire whisk. Add the cucumbers, garlic, mint, and salt, and combine. Garnish with a fresh mint leaf if desired. Serve cold.

Green Beans and Tomato Stew
(Loobieh Bel-Zeit)

YIELD: 8 SERVINGS

This dish is made by thousands of Lebanese homemakers on a weekly basis with some regional variations. In some communities, the tomatoes are omitted—not unusual, considering that tomatoes were not indigenous to the region. This dish is served at room temperature and often ordered at a mezze. It can be a frugal and delicious dinner on a balmy summer evening, along with pita bread, sliced radishes, and a few olives.

Directions:

1) Heat the oil in a Dutch oven over medium heat and sauté the onions until they turn golden, about 15 minutes. Add the green beans, lower the heat, and sauté them alongside the onions, stirring from time to time, about 30 minutes. The beans need to get soft.

2) Add the garlic paste, the whole garlic cloves, tomatoes, chili pepper (if using), salt, and white pepper to the skillet and stir a bit to combine. Cover and simmer gently, until the green beans are cooked and well-softened, about 35 minutes.

3) Simmer uncovered an additional 15 minutes if the beans are not meltingly soft or if there is too much tomato juice in the pot. When the juice has almost completely evaporated, turn off the heat and set the skillet aside to cool. Transfer the veggies to a serving platter and serve at room temperature with pita bread on the side.

NOTE: *In the States, I prefer to use frozen green beans to save time. To make peeling the garlic cloves easier, dunk them in boiling water for 5 seconds and drain them. The peel will come right off.*

Meat Version of This Dish:

This dish may also be prepared with meat (stew meat or lamb shanks) and served hot with rice. Brown half a pound of meat pieces first, then add a quart of water and simmer for a couple of hours until the meat is tender. Add the tomatoes or ½ cup of tomato paste halfway through. Add the green beans 30 minutes before the end of cooking. Add the garlic paste, whole garlic cloves, salt, and pepper, and simmer for another 15 minutes. Taste, adjust seasoning, and serve with a rice pilaf.

Ingredients:

1 cup olive oil

2 pounds onions, chopped

2 pounds green beans *(fresh or frozen)*. If fresh, snap off the stringy ends and cut the beans in half or, if desired, lengthwise as well *(this will make them very thin and release their flavor)*

1 tablespoon garlic paste *(see Chapter 2, "Basics")*

1 head of garlic, cloves peeled and kept whole

2 pounds fresh vine tomatoes or best-quality Italian canned *(32 ounces)* tomatoes, chopped

1 red chili pepper *(optional)*, kept whole and added to the stew to give it heat if desired *(can substitute 1 tablespoon hot red pepper paste)*

Salt, to taste

½ teaspoon white pepper

Salads and Sides

Tomatoes with Sumac Dressing
(Banadoora Bel-Summak)

YIELD: 4 SERVINGS

Ingredients:

4 large tomatoes
*(any variety, but
preferably heirloom)*

1 tablespoon sumac

1 teaspoon garlic paste
(see Chapter 2, "Basics")

1 medium lemon, juiced
(about 3 tablespoons)

½ cup olive oil

Tomatoes are so popular in the Lebanese diet, it is hard to believe that they are new to the country. According to Dr. Helou, nutrition expert and head of that department at Saint Joseph University in Beirut, tomatoes were introduced by way of Asia through the Silk Road trade route. Tomatoes are served sliced on a plate with just about every course. A prized variety of tomatoes in Lebanon, called *jabalieh* from *jabal* (the word for "mountain"), starts appearing at the end of May on every roadside climbing up to mountain villages. These tomatoes are huge, meaty, and full of flavor. A traditional way to dress them is with this simple sumac dressing. Sumac grows wild all over the mountains in Lebanon, is dried and powdered, and sprinkled on veggies or eggs for that lemony flavor.

Directions:

Slice the tomatoes. Whisk the sumac, garlic paste, lemon juice, and oil in a salad bowl with a fork until combined. Pour on the tomatoes and serve.

Potato Cubes with Cilantro Pesto
(Batata Harra)

YIELD: 4 SERVINGS

This is the one item on a mezze menu in Lebanon I will always order. I just think the combo of potatoes, cilantro, garlic, and hot pepper is dynamite! Try it once and you will be hooked.

Taste of Beirut

Directions:

1) Peel the potatoes and dice them into small pieces, about half an inch in width. Place them in a bowl of cold water until all are cut.

2) In a large skillet, heat the oil to 375 degrees F. Drain, pat the potatoes dry, and fry until golden. Remove from the skillet and place on a plate lined with paper towels to absorb the extra oil.

3) Transfer the hot oil to a bowl and place the cilantro pesto in the skillet; it should sizzle a few seconds. Transfer the potatoes back to the skillet and gently toss to combine with the cilantro pesto. Sprinkle the hot pepper powder all over and toss gently to mix. Serve with quartered lemons on the side.

Ingredients:

1½ pounds potatoes (*Yukon Gold or similar*) or taro

3¼ cups olive oil or a combo of olive oil and vegetable oil

2 packages cilantro pesto (*see Chapter 2, "Basics"*)

1 teaspoon hot pepper powder or 1 jalapeño pepper, seeded and chopped fine (*optional*)

1 small lemon, quartered

NOTE: *This dish is perfect with taro as well. It may be found fresh in US supermarkets, as well as cut up and frozen in Middle Eastern grocery stores. Taro needs to be soaked in lemony water after peeling, or it will turn black.*

Lighter version of the same dish:

1) After draining the potatoes, in a Dutch oven, heat ½ cup water and ½ cup oil over medium-high heat. Place the potatoes in the pot and cover tightly. Let the potatoes steam and cook for about 15 to 20 minutes, shaking the pot from time to time to prevent scorching. When the potatoes are cooked, turn the heat off and set the pot aside.

1) In a skillet, heat 6 tablespoons of olive oil, add the cilantro pesto, and sauté for 10 seconds until fragrant. Transfer the potatoes to the skillet and gently combine them with the pesto. Add the chili pepper or jalapeño pepper, if using. The idea is to get the potatoes coated with the pesto as much as possible. Serve warm or at room temperature with quartered lemons.

Salads and Sides

Classic Tabbouleh Salad

YIELD: 4 TO 8 SERVINGS

This salad is considered Lebanon's national dish. There is now a National Tabbouleh Day in the country, with a contest held at Souk el Tayeb, Beirut's organic open-air market. Tabbouleh is always present at a Lebanese mezze table. According to the Lebanese Gastronomy Association, there are several components that make up an authentic tabbouleh: flat-leaf parsley, bulgur, tomatoes, onion, olive oil, and lemon juice. Parsley is the main ingredient in tabbouleh, while bulgur is just sprinkled, as an accent. Parsley in Lebanon is extremely soft and silky, which is what makes this a most enjoyable salad. Cucumbers are *never* included in tabbouleh.

Regarding tabbouleh, I asked Dr. Helou, head of the Nutrition Department at Saint Joseph University in Beirut, what dish he had most often at home. His response was immediate: "Tabbouleh, every day!" He told me that a world public health expert, Dr. Nicole Darmon, had done several studies and concluded that tabbouleh was the world's healthiest dish.

Directions:

1) Wash and dry the parsley and mint, picking out the leaves and discarding the stems. Chop the leaves very fine, by hand preferably.

2) Chop the onion and peel and dice the tomatoes, reserving the juice.

3) Soak the bulgur in water or a mixture of water and the reserved tomato juice for 20 minutes. Drain and squeeze well.

4) For the dressing, whisk the lemon juice in a bowl with the oil, salt, and allspice.

5) Toss the parsley, mint, onions, tomatoes, and bulgur in a bowl with the dressing. Serve.

Ingredients:

3 bunches Italian parsley

1 bunch fresh mint

1 large white onion or 1 bunch green onions, chopped

3 large heirloom tomatoes

¼ cup bulgur *(fine grade, #1)*

½ cup fresh lemon juice

½ cup olive oil *(add more if desired)*

½ teaspoon salt

½ teaspoon allspice

Romaine lettuce *(inner leaves to scoop out the salad)*, cabbage leaves, or fresh grape leaves

Salads and Sides

NOTE: *If you are making the tabbouleh in advance, add the dressing at the last moment to avoid wilting the herbs. Heirloom tomatoes are the best to use, but any other variety is fine as long as the tomatoes are ripe and meaty; replace with double the amount of tomatoes if using Roma tomatoes, for example.*

Eggplant and Peppers Salad
(Al-Raheb)

YIELD: 4 SERVINGS

This salad is named after an unknown monk. Presumably, he lived in one of the monasteries that pepper the Lebanese mountains. Like all monks, he lived a frugal life, eating whatever vegetables his plot of land produced (which was the case for most Lebanese mountain folks and not just monks!). In any case, this is a refreshing and delicious salad that is usually part of the offerings at a mezze. I had it at the beach one year, and it was just a perfect dish for the setting.

Ingredients:

1½ pounds eggplant

1 cup chopped Italian parsley

3 green onions, chopped fine

4 medium tomatoes, diced small

1 green bell pepper, seeded and diced small (*can include bits of a red bell pepper in the mix, if desired*)

Dressing:

¾ cup olive oil

½ cup lemon juice

1 tablespoon pomegranate molasses

1 teaspoon garlic paste (*see Chapter 2, "Basics"*)

Salt, if needed

Directions:

1) Peel, slice, and salt the eggplant. Place the slices in a colander and let them sweat out the brownish liquid for 30 minutes or so. Preheat the oven to 350 degrees F. Wipe the slices dry and transfer them to a baking sheet sprayed with cooking oil. Brush the slices with olive oil. Bake for 20 minutes until soft.

2) In a small bowl, whisk the dressing ingredients until combined. Taste and adjust seasoning.

3) Dice the eggplant and transfer to a salad bowl. Add the other ingredients and pour the dressing over the bowl; toss lightly. Serve at room temperature with a basket of pita bread if desired.

NOTE: *The eggplant can be charred over an open flame, peeled, and mashed, or it can be grilled; any of these methods will work with this salad.*

Salads and Sides

Potato Salad *(Salatet Batata)*

YIELD: 4 SERVINGS

Ingredients:

1 pound waxy potatoes
  (such as Yukon Gold)

½ cup fresh lemon juice

½ cup extra-virgin olive oil

1 teaspoon sea salt, or
  to taste

1 cup fresh, finely chopped
  Italian parsley

A Lebanese-style potato salad is extremely simple to make and requires only three ingredients besides the potatoes: lemons, extra-virgin olive oil, and parsley. The potatoes should be firm and buttery rather than the starchy baking potatoes. The resulting salad is tangy from the lemon, a bit peppery from the parsley, and creamy from the olive oil, but altogether light and satisfying.

Directions:

Boil the potatoes (or steam them) until tender. Peel and dice into small pieces, no more than half an inch in width. Transfer them to a bowl. Pour the fresh lemon juice onto the potatoes, tossing gently to combine. Add the oil and sprinkle with the salt and parsley. Toss to mix well and serve at room temperature.

CHAPTER 6

Main Courses

A Lebanese proverb states,
"Hunger turns you into a nonbeliever,
doubting God" *(Al-jaw' kaafer)*.
This chapter begins with a selection of
simple and easy meals that will quickly
assuage your hunger and keep
you out of trouble!

STEWS

Stews *(yakhneh)* are the main meal of the day and epitomize homestyle cooking. A Lebanese stew usually showcases one main vegetable, gently simmered with meat (lamb shanks or beef), and served with a rice pilaf. Lebanon imports most of its meat, except for the half a million or so goats roaming the mountains and valleys.

RICE, GRAINS, AND LEGUMES

Bulgur and lentils are revered in the traditional Lebanese provincial culture, which refers to them both as "nails to the knees" *(masameer el-rekbeh)*. In other words, these foods are believed to provide strength and stamina. Scientific research in nutrition has confirmed these beliefs, for the protein, fiber, and mineral content of these foods surpass most others. In the past, Lebanese farmers grew their own wheat and manually processed bulgur in the community. Rice, introduced to the country from Asia, became widely popular, giving rise to a proverb, "Rice took the prize and bulgur hung himself in despair" *(al ʾezz lal-ruz w al-berghol shanak halo)*. Despite the popularity of rice, bulgur is here to stay and is a main component of kibbeh, Lebanon's national dish. Kibbeh is simply a paste obtained by combining fine bulgur with lean meat; during fasting or lean times, kibbeh is made with vegetables (such as potato or pumpkin) and called "sad" or "tricky" kibbeh.

KIBBEH

Kibbeh is the food that the Lebanese have been most successful at exporting overseas. In Brazil or the Dominican Republic, kibbeh is called *kibe* and has been adopted as a native food. While kibbeh made with meat is the most popular, in the Chouf Mountains, local folks have made kibbeh with wild porcupine *(enfud)* meat, a supposedly exquisitely tender kibbeh. Around the world, innovative chefs have created kibbeh dishes with salmon or seafood. In Lebanon, the consensus is to stick to tradition; meat or pumpkin kibbeh balls are served at a *mezze* and kibbeh pies at formal meals. In the olden days kibbeh meat was pounded by hand in a huge stone mortar *(jeren)* and any silver skin would be pulled out by hand; as a result, the meat paste was as smooth as silk. Nowadays, to save time and effort, kibbeh meat is processed in a meat grinder or a food processor.

SEAFOOD DISHES

Lebanon is flanked on its west side by a 140-mile long strip of Mediterranean coastline. Three of the most populated cities in the country (Beirut, Sidon in the south, and Tripoli in the north) are coastal cities, and each claims the creation of a famous seafood dish. By and large, fish, when freshly caught, is simply baked or fried and enjoyed with a *tarator* sauce on the side, along with fried pita chips.

Mock Kibbeh Tartare
(Begin with Muhammara)

YIELD: 8 SERVINGS

The requirements for a traditional kibbeh tartare are not very conducive to modern urban living. The trusted butcher should have slaughtered the animal that same day and the meat should be scrupulously cleaned, with goat meat being the recommended meat. Therefore, the alternative is to make what looks like kibbeh tartare—without a drop of meat.

The ensconced habit in Lebanon, when one cannot have meat (due to fasting or lack of resources), is to call these dishes "tricky kibbeh," "liar kibbeh," or "sad kibbeh"; the attitude is to just pretend! I stumbled on this dish when I was home, hungry, and wanted to eat within minutes. I found a bowl of prepared muhammara (red pepper dip) in the fridge and thought of combining it with some bulgur. The result was flavorful and the effort was minimal.

Ingredients:

1½ cups bulgur *(#1 or #2)*

3 cups boiling water

¾ cup prepared red pepper dip *(see Red Pepper and Walnut Dip on p. 124)*

1 teaspoon salt, or to taste

½ teaspoon black pepper

1 bunch fresh basil or mint leaves

1 bunch green onions, kept whole

1 bunch radishes, sliced

½ cup olive oil

Directions:

Soak the bulgur in the boiling water and add the red pepper dip, salt, and pepper. Cook until tender, about 15 minutes, or until the bulgur has totally absorbed the water and has melded with the red pepper dip. Taste to adjust seasoning. Transfer the mixture to a platter, spreading it out carefully with a spatula. Garnish with fresh basil or mint and serve with green onions and radishes. Drizzle olive oil on the kibbeh prior to serving. Serve at room temperature or slightly warm.

NOTE: *Traditional kibbeh tartare made with meat is spooned on a piece of pita bread, drizzled with olive oil, and eaten with a chunk of raw onion or scallion and some fresh mint leaves. If you make the red pepper dip from scratch for this recipe, skip adding the bread crumbs and use only half the batch.*

Meals in a Jiffy

Kafta Pie with Tarator Sauce

YIELD: 4 SERVINGS

This dish is made with kafta paste topped with tarator sauce and baked. Kafta is a seasoned meat mixture (a type of Lebanese meat loaf) prepared by butcher shops in Lebanon. Kafta can be prepared with a food processor in minutes at home.

Ingredients:

1 onion, quartered

1 cup finely chopped Italian parsley *(chop by hand first)*

1 pound ground beef or a mixture of ground beef and ground lamb *(preferably extra lean)*

1 teaspoon salt

1 teaspoon allspice

½ teaspoon cinnamon

2 cups tarator sauce *(see Chapter 2, "Basics," double the recipe)*

¼ cup fried or toasted pine nuts or sliced almonds *(see "Nuts" in Chapter 2, "Basics")*

French fries, for serving

Directions:

1) Place the onion in a food processor with the parsley. Pulse a few times until the onion is chopped fine and mixed with the parsley. Add the meat, salt, allspice, and cinnamon, and process until the mixture is well combined and pasty. Transfer to a greased ovenproof pan (such as a 9-inch pie plate or oblong plate) and pat it to spread it evenly.

2) Heat the oven to 350 degrees F. Spread the tarator sauce over the kafta. Bake for 20 minutes or until the kafta is thoroughly cooked. Sprinkle the pine nuts or almonds on the surface of the kafta. Serve with french fries.

NOTE: *I use an oblong dish, but any dish will do, including a 9-inch pie plate or a standard loaf pan. The baking time will simply need to be adjusted. I always like to mix ground lamb with the ground beef because the lamb makes it more moist (and fattier).*

Meals in a Jiffy

Bulgur with Tomatoes Pilaf
(Burghul Bel-Banadoora)

YIELD: 8 SERVINGS

This dish uses up the last glorious tomatoes of the season. The bulgur drinks up the tomato juice while cooking and develops a mild tomato taste and a silky texture. Some people add diced green peppers to the pilaf; I prefer to stick with the pure tomato taste.

   This is a good choice as a side dish for a sit-down dinner or a buffet party (one tomato per person). Normally, it is served on a large platter at family gatherings. Spooning it into tomato shells makes this humble dish look fancy. Despite the absence of meat, and its simplicity, this dish is hearty and filling.

Directions:

1) Cut the tomato caps off and set aside. Using a serrated grapefruit spoon, empty the contents of the tomatoes into a bowl. Puree the tomato flesh in a blender or food processor. Sprinkle the hollow tomatoes with salt and flip them onto a cutting board to drain as much as possible. Place them on a serving plate and set aside. Carefully pour the juice off the cutting board into a bowl with the tomato puree.

2) Heat the oil in a Dutch oven set over medium heat. Sauté the onions until soft, about 10 minutes. Add the bulgur and stir a couple of minutes until all the grains are shiny. Sprinkle with the spices. Pour the tomato puree, the tomato paste (if needed), and the water over the grains. Bring to a boil, cover, and lower the heat. Simmer for about 20 minutes.

3) Uncover the pot and adjust the seasoning, if necessary. Check the texture of the bulgur. If it's soft and silky, it's done. If it is still hard, add ½ cup more water and cook a bit longer. Cool.

4) Scoop the pilaf into the hollowed-out tomatoes, place the tomato caps on top, and put the extra pilaf all around the serving plate. Serve warm or at room temperature.

Ingredients:

2 pounds red and juicy tomatoes *(or a 24-ounce can of good quality tomatoes; reserve the juice)*

1½ teaspoons salt

½ cup olive oil

2 medium onions, chopped fine

1½ cups bulgur *(medium or coarse, #3 or #4)*

1 teaspoon allspice or 1 teaspoon ground caraway

3 cups water

2 tablespoons tomato paste diluted with the extra tomato juice or water, if needed *(see note below)*

NOTE: *If the tomatoes are not very juicy or flavorful, adding the tomato paste will intensify the flavor of this dish. One of my friends, Hoda, swears that the addition of caraway is essential for giving this dish depth of flavor. Caraway also fights bloating.*

Meals in a Jiffy

Grilled Fish Fillet with Walnut Sauce

YIELD: 4 SERVINGS

Ingredients:

½ cup olive oil

½ cup lemon juice

1 teaspoon salt *(or to taste)*

1 teaspoon cinnamon powder

½ teaspoon white pepper

1½ pounds white fish fillets

½ cup chopped Italian parsley

2 cinnamon sticks *(cut in two lengthwise)*

Walnut sauce *(see Chapter 2, "Basics")*

Directions:

Preheat the broiler to medium-low. Put the oil, lemon juice, salt, cinnamon, and pepper into a bowl and whisk to combine. Place the fish fillets on a foil-lined baking pan and drizzle the sauce over the fish. Sprinkle the parsley on the fish and tuck the cinnamon sticks in between. Cover with foil and bake gently for 12 minutes or until the fish flakes easily when poked with a fork. Serve with the walnut sauce.

Meals in a Jiffy

Grilled Lamb Chops
with Mashed Sweet Potatoes

YIELD: 4 SERVINGS

Directions:

1) Sprinkle the chops with salt, pepper, and thyme, and place in a greased baking dish.

2) Mix the lemon juice and oil in a bowl and pour it over the chops. Cover and marinate the chops for 30 minutes or overnight in the refrigerator.

3) Peel the sweet potatoes and put them in a saucepan. Cover them with water and bring to a boil. Lower the heat and simmer for 30 minutes until the potatoes are thoroughly cooked.

4) Drain the chops and pat them dry. Grill over medium-hot coals or panfry over medium heat for 3 minutes on each side. Put the chops on a serving dish and keep them warm while preparing the sweet potatoes.

5) Drain the sweet potatoes and mash them in a bowl. Add the tarator sauce to the sweet potatoes, mixing to combine, and taste to adjust seasoning. The amount of tarator will depend on the amount of potatoes. A rule of thumb is not to use too much, as it is overpowering. Ultimately, though, it is a matter of taste.

6) Serve the chops with the mashed sweet potatoes dressed with the tarator sauce.

Ingredients:

8 lamb chops

1 teaspoon salt

½ teaspoon black pepper or white pepper

1 teaspoon fresh thyme or oregano

¼ cup lemon juice

¼ cup olive oil

4 medium sweet potatoes

½ cup to 1 cup tarator sauce *(see Chapter 2, "Basics")*

NOTE: *You may use a basic tarator sauce for this recipe or use citrus-tahini sauce (see Chapter 2, "Basics" for recipe). For a pretty presentation, bake the sweet potatoes in the microwave, spoon out the pulp, mix with the tarator sauce, taste to season, and spoon the mashed sweet potatoes back into the sweet potato skins. I would also suggest making a tarator with some orange juice mixed with the lemon juice. You could serve the leftover sauce on the side as well.*

Meals in a Jiffy

Eggplant Cake
(Yvette's *Maghmoor*)

YIELD: 8 SERVINGS

This eggplant cake is a showstopper. It is perfect for a buffet, is served at room temperature, is vegan, and is simple to prepare. This recipe is from Mrs. Yvette Tabet, who grew up in Egypt as a Lebanese when it was a British colony (many Lebanese immigrated to Egypt back then, my grandfather among them). She told me this recipe was her grandmother's, so I estimate it is around 150 years old. I streamlined the steps, as the original recipe takes three days to make. This was common back then, as available help was plentiful with every household outfitted with many helpers—each assigned a specific task—and a housekeeper. I've duly revised the recipe, and it will take you no more than one hour from start to finish.

Ingredients:

2 pounds eggplant, cut into ¼-inch slices and sprinkled with salt

½ cup oil

2 medium onions, sliced

1½ pounds tomatoes, chopped

1 can *(15.5 ounces)* chickpeas, drained and rinsed

1 teaspoon allspice

½ teaspoon black pepper

Salt, to taste

1 cup tomato puree

Directions:

1) Heat the oven to 450 degrees F. Lay the eggplant slices on a baking sheet sprayed with cooking oil. Spray the tops of the eggplant slices. Bake until soft and browned. (Watch the eggplants closely to make sure they don't burn.) Remove the eggplant from the oven and reduce the oven temperature to 325 degrees F.

2) Heat the oil over medium heat in a large skillet and sauté the onions until soft. Add the tomatoes, chickpeas, allspice, pepper, and salt. Simmer gently for 15 minutes, adding a bit of water to prevent the mixture from scorching the skillet.

3) Line a 9-inch springform pan with foil, wax paper, or baking paper. Cover the bottom with the eggplant slices, overlapping them so that no gap is visible. Top the eggplants with the onion, tomato, and chickpea mixture. Cover with the remaining eggplant slices.

4) Pour the tomato puree over the surface. Bake for 20 minutes. Cool the cake on the counter, then cover and refrigerate. Before serving, bring the cake to room temperature, remove from the mold, and serve.

Meals in a Jiffy

Wings, Lebanese-Style

YIELD: 4 SERVINGS

Do you have any idea what distinguishes a Lebanese home kitchen? The whiff of fried garlic and cilantro, that's what. Chicken wings get the garlic and cilantro treatment with the addition of a squeeze of fresh lemon juice the last couple minutes of cooking.

Ingredients:

1 pound chicken wings *(not deboned)*

2 lemons or more, 1 juiced, and the other cut into quarters

½ cup flour *(optional)*

1 teaspoon dried coriander

1 teaspoon salt

½ teaspoon white pepper or black pepper

3 cups oil

1 cilantro pesto package from the freezer, or make fresh cilantro pesto *(see Chapter 2, "Basics")*

Directions:

1) Clean the wings under running water by rubbing them with a cut lemon quarter. Dry them with paper towels and sprinkle them with flour, coriander, salt, and pepper. Heat the oil in a Dutch oven and brown the wings on all sides for about 40 minutes. Drain the oil from the wings.

2) Add one batch of cilantro pesto to the wings and toss to coat (add more if desired). Drizzle lemon juice all over them. Transfer the wings to a serving platter and serve with the remaining lemon quarters.

Meals in a Jiffy

Pasta with Yogurt Sauce

YIELD: 4 SERVINGS

Ingredients:

8 ounces dry pasta *(small penne, elbow, or small tube-shaped)*

1 tablespoon vegetable oil

16 ounces plain organic yogurt

¼ cup tahini

1 teaspoon garlic paste *(see Chapter 2, "Basics")*

1 teaspoon salt, to taste

1 teaspoon allspice

¼ cup toasted pine nuts or sliced almonds *(see "Nuts" in Chapter 2, "Basics")*

A classic of Lebanese home cooking, this pasta and sauce is usually prepared without meat. It is ideal for warm days because the yogurt sauce is not cooked. It is a perfect meal for any day of the week when cooking elaborate meals is the last thing on the agenda.

Directions:

1) Cook the pasta as directed on the package. Drain, pour into a bowl, and drizzle the oil over the pasta and toss.

2) Mix the yogurt, tahini, garlic paste, salt, and allspice in a small bowl. Taste and adjust seasoning. Pour the sauce over the pasta and mix to combine well. Garnish with the pine nuts or almond slices. Serve.

VARIATION: Another version of this pasta includes the addition of boiled green fava or lima beans and omits the tahini, instead swirling cilantro pesto in the yogurt sauce right before serving.

Meals in a Jiffy

Pasta with Red Lentil Sauce

YIELD: 4 SERVINGS

Ingredients:

⅓ cup olive oil

8 ounces penne *(or any shape of dry pasta, the smaller the better)*

4 cups chicken stock, boiling hot

1 cup red lentils

1 cup carrot coins *(frozen or fresh)*

1 tablespoon garlic paste *(see Chapter 2, "Basics")*

1 teaspoon cumin

1 tablespoon red pepper paste *(or 1 teaspoon chili powder)*

¼ cup chopped fresh parsley, optional

My nineteen-year-old came home famished and inquired about food. What's a mama to do? I whipped up some pasta with a red lentil sauce, and we were both satiated thirty minutes later. This is loosely inspired by the Egyptian *koshari*.

Directions:

Heat the oil in a Dutch oven. Add the pasta and stir-fry until coated with oil and slightly toasted. Add the chicken stock, lentils, carrots, garlic paste, cumin, and red pepper paste. Bring to a boil and cover the pan. Let the mixture boil for 15 minutes or until the pasta has absorbed all the water and is cooked. Adjust seasoning and serve.

NOTE: *The pasta with the lentils will dry out when cool. This is a dish best served while still warm. If it dries out too much when cooled down, add a little bit of water when reheating it in the microwave and stir.*

Meals in a Jiffy

Ground Meat and Potato Hash
(Mfarket el-Batata)

YIELD: 4 SERVINGS

Finger-licking good and very versatile! There are many versions of *mfarket* (meaning "rubbed") in the rural Lebanese cuisine repertoire, some with eggs baked on top of veggies, some without. This one is hard to resist with fried potatoes, rubbed with browned meat and onions.

Ingredients:

1½ pounds potatoes *(Yukon Gold or a similar variety are best)*

2 cups plus 2 tablespoons olive oil

1 large onion, chopped

⅓ pound ground beef

1 teaspoon salt

1 teaspoon allspice

½ teaspoon black pepper

½ teaspoon cinnamon

Dash of ground nutmeg

¼ cup water or stock

¼ cup chopped parsley, for garnish

Directions:

1) Peel and dice the potatoes and soak in a bowl of water. Set aside.

2) Heat 2 tablespoons of the oil in a skillet and sauté the onion until golden. Brown the meat in the same skillet, separating it to keep it from forming big lumps. Add the salt, allspice, pepper, cinnamon, and nutmeg, and stir to combine.

3) Drain the potatoes and pat dry on kitchen towels. Heat the remaining oil to 375 degrees F in a deep saucepan and fry the potatoes until crispy and golden. Drain them of most of the oil and transfer them to the skillet with the meat and onion mixture, stirring a bit to combine. Add the water, cover the skillet, lower the heat, and cook the mixture for 3 minutes. Uncover, sprinkle with parsley, and serve.

Meals in a Jiffy

Chickpeas with Cumin (Balila)

YIELD: 4 SERVINGS

This is a very simple dish served at all the neighborhood eateries in Beirut for breakfast (starting at 6:00 AM) and brunch or in cafés as part of a mezze. The chickpeas are slowly simmered for hours and dressed with cumin, olive oil, and not much else. It is served with pita bread and the usual trimmings of fresh onion slices, sliced tomatoes, fresh mint sprigs, and olives and pickles. The secret to this recipe is the quality of the chickpeas. A famous *balila* maker in Beirut told me he gets his chickpeas from Mexico, in 100-pound bags. Apparently the ones growing in the Bekaa Valley in Lebanon are too scrawny for his (high) standards. The chickpeas, as they slowly simmer, become softer and softer. Dressed with olive oil, mashed garlic, and a sprinkle of ground cumin, they melt in the mouth and are irresistible. Served with pita bread and trimmings, it is people's food at its finest.

Ingredients:

2 cans *(15.5 ounces each)* garbanzo beans

¾ cup extra-virgin olive oil

1 tablespoon garlic paste *(see Chapter 2, "Basics")*

1½ teaspoons ground cumin, more to taste

Salt, to taste

Directions:

Rinse the beans, put them in a pot, and add enough water to cover them. Add the oil, garlic paste, cumin, and salt, and mix well. Simmer for 30 minutes over low heat, mashing the chickpeas here and there until they form a thick and soupy mixture. Serve warm with extra cumin and olive oil. Eat with pita and fresh radishes, green onions, fresh mint sprigs, pickles, and olives, if desired.

NOTE: *Balila can be served for a mezze dressed with more seasonings if desired, such as garlic paste, lemon juice, and a dash of cinnamon. Of course, one can make it with the dry chickpeas, in which case they need to be soaked in plenty of water overnight, drained, covered in water, and simmered gently until soft.*

Meals in a Jiffy

Lamb in Yogurt Sauce
(Laban Ummo)

YIELD: 4 SERVINGS

Laban is "yogurt" in Arabic and *ummo* is "mother." This is a dish of virginal tenderness: the creamy yogurt sauce and the silky tenderness of the lamb shanks contribute to a gustatory experience of absolute purity. Tradition calls for preparing this dish on New Year's Day to symbolically start the year on a good footing.

Directions:

1) Put the lamb shanks, onion, bay leaf, cinnamon stick, allspice, peppercorns, salt, and 4 cups of the water in a large Dutch oven. Bring the stock to a simmer, skimming the froth from the top, and cook over gentle heat until the lamb shanks become tender and fall off the bone. Remove the shanks and set aside. Boil the stock (if necessary) until it is reduced to approximately 2 cups. Strain and reserve the stock in a bowl.

2) Put the cooked yogurt sauce in the Dutch oven over medium heat. Pour the meat stock over the yogurt sauce while stirring, and bring the sauce to a simmer. Thicken the sauce with the cornstarch mixture, stirring it constantly.

3) Meanwhile, heat the oil or butter in a skillet over medium heat and lightly brown the pearl onions on all sides. Add the remaining water to the onions and simmer gently until the water has evaporated.

4) Separate the lamb pieces, discarding the fat and cartilage. Place the lamb pieces and the pearl onions in the pot with the yogurt sauce. Serve with rice and vermicelli pilaf (see Chapter 2, "Basics").

Ingredients:

1 pound lamb shanks (shaved in 2-inch chunks)

1 large yellow onion, quartered

1 bay leaf

1 cinnamon stick

3 allspice berries

4 peppercorns

1 tablespoon salt

5 cups cold water

1 batch cooked yogurt sauce (see Chapter 2, "Basics")

2 tablespoons cornstarch diluted in ⅓ cup water

2 tablespoons oil or clarified butter

1 pound pearl onions

1 batch rice and vermicelli pilaf (see Chapter 2, "Basics")

NOTE: *The large yellow onion is to use for the lamb shanks when making the lamb stock; the others get cooked separately and served with the yogurt sauce and meat pieces at the end.*

NOTE: *For a meatless version, replace the meat with a bag of frozen green fava beans. At home, my grandmother would flavor this stew with mint pesto (refer to Chapter 2, "Basics"); however, a lot of folks serve it plain just as is. Other versions include adding three or four mastic stones (ground up with a dash of salt) to the yogurt and meat stew the last five minutes of cooking. You can also replace the allspice and peppercorns with ground spices if that is what is available in your spice pantry.*

Stews and Stuffed Veggies

Carrot and Pea Stew
(Yakhnet al-Bazella w-Jazar)

YIELD: 4 SERVINGS

Lebanese expats (at least the ones I have met) like to reminisce fondly about the *yakhneh* (stew) of their mother or grandmother. A large portion of the Lebanese culinary repertoire is dedicated to these yakhneh, encompassing every vegetable under the sun and almost always with the same basic formula: a stock made of lamb shanks (or beef) cut in small pieces, a final flavoring of cilantro pesto or mint pesto, and rice and vermicelli pilaf as a side with the stew. We had them several times a week at home, with different vegetables. Unlike stews in the West, which comprise a medley of vegetables, stews in Lebanese cuisine showcase one vegetable, such as spinach, green beans, okra, beans, zucchini, artichokes, and so on—the list is nearly endless.

Ingredients:

3 tablespoons oil

1 pound beef or lamb stew meat

½ cup tomato paste *(or 1 pound tomatoes, peeled, diced, and pureed in a blender)*

6 cups water

1 large onion, chopped

1 bay leaf

3 sprigs parsley

1 teaspoon cinnamon

1 teaspoon allspice

1 teaspoon salt

½ teaspoon black pepper

1 pound carrots, peeled and sliced

½ pound frozen sweet peas *(or fresh peas)*

1 cilantro pesto packet *(see Chapter 2, "Basics")*

Directions:

1) Heat the oil in a Dutch oven and brown the meat pieces on all sides, about 10 minutes. Add the tomato paste and water (or the pureed tomatoes and enough water to add up to 6 cups), as well as the onion, bay leaf, parsley, cinnamon, allspice, salt, and pepper and cover the pot. Bring to a boil, lower the heat, and simmer. After 20 minutes, add the carrots. Skim any froth from the surface with a spatula. Add the peas the last 10 minutes of cooking.

2) Add the cilantro pesto the last 5 minutes of cooking; taste to adjust seasoning and serve with rice pilaf on the side.

Stews and Stuffed Veggies

Walnut and Chicken Stew
(Circassian Chicken Sharkasieh)

YIELD: 8 SERVINGS

The very first time that I ever heard of Circassians was in Dallas. I met a lady who told me (in Arabic) that she was a Circassian from Jordan. I was hoping my blank look did not give away the fact that I wasn't familiar with the term. Circassians are a North Caucasian ethnic group who were dispossessed and took refuge in the Middle East. This dish (also known as *shebs-wabasta*) is attributed to their community. Walnuts paired with red pepper paste are a heavenly match, and it is one of my favorite taste combos, especially when using red pepper with a bit of heat. The dish is rich, but since walnuts are supposed to be so nutritious, I'd allow an occasional indulgence. A traditional accompaniment for this dish is rice and bulgur pilaf *(see Chapter 2, "Basics")*. This recipe is from chef Fikriyeh Hassan in Beirut.

Directions:

1) Place the chicken in a Dutch oven. Cover with water and add the clove-studded onion, bay leaf, carrot, and peppercorns. Bring to a gentle simmer, skimming any froth from the surface, until the chicken is cooked. Remove the chicken and transfer it to a large cutting board, reserving the broth. Cool the chicken and cut it into large pieces.

2) Strain the broth and pour it back into the Dutch oven. Simmer the broth for a while to reduce it to 3 cups. Add the bread, walnuts, quartered onion, garlic paste, red pepper paste, whipping cream, and coriander. Simmer the sauce gently for 20 minutes.

3) Using an immersion blender (or transfer the mixture to a regular blender), puree the mixture until smooth. Taste and adjust seasoning. Simmer a while longer if the broth is too runny; it needs to have body and be thick, yet creamy, like yogurt.

4) Put the chicken into the broth, let bubbles burst for a few seconds, and serve warm rice.

Ingredients:

1 chicken *(3 pounds)*, sprinkled with salt

2 onions, one quartered, the other studded with whole cloves

1 bay leaf

1 carrot

6 black peppercorns

6 slices whole-wheat sandwich bread

2 cups toasted walnuts *(see "Nuts" in Chapter 2, "Basics")*

2 tablespoons garlic paste *(see Chapter 2, "Basics")*

½ cup red pepper paste *(available in all Middle Eastern markets)*

1 cup whipping cream

1 teaspoon ground coriander

NOTE: *Instead of adding the red pepper paste to the chicken broth, you can heat ¼ cup oil in a small skillet, add the red pepper paste, and let it sizzle. Add it to the broth at the end of cooking to form pretty red swirls. The red pepper paste can be hot or mild or a mixture of the two. The chicken can be browned in the pot, then covered with water to make the broth. This will give the stew an even richer flavor.*

Stews and Stuffed Veggies

Spinach and Ground Beef Stew
(Yakhnet el-Sabanekh)

YIELD: 4 SERVINGS

This stew is, for me, the epitome of Lebanese home cooking. It is extremely plain—just spinach, a little meat, and some garlic and spices. However, it is very good and really does a fine job of showcasing spinach.

If you can, use fresh spinach, preferably organic. Spinach comes already cleaned in bags in US supermarkets, which saves time. In Lebanon, it takes a good 15 minutes of rinsing multiple times to get rid of the dirt, and even after all this labor, a healthy worm is found nestled on a leaf. (However, fresh veggies taste wonderful there.)

Chop and use the spinach stems as well. The stew is served with rice and quartered lemons. Lentils, mung beans, or chickpeas, previously cooked, could be substituted for the meat and would make this a vegetarian meal.

Ingredients:

¼ cup olive oil

2 large onions, chopped

1 pound ground beef

1 teaspoon salt

½ teaspoon black pepper

1 teaspoon allspice

½ teaspoon cinnamon

1 cup water

4 bunches fresh spinach, rinsed several times and chopped fine with the stems *(or 3 ten-ounce boxes frozen chopped spinach) (about 2 pounds)*

1 tablespoon garlic paste *(see Chapter 2, "Basics")*

3 large lemons, 1 juiced *(¼ cup juice)* and 2 quartered

Directions:

1) Heat the olive oil in a Dutch oven over medium heat and sauté the onions until golden. Add the meat and brown it, breaking it apart with two wooden spoons to keep the pieces small. Season with the salt, pepper, allspice, and cinnamon.

2) Add the water and spinach. Stir a bit and cover the pot while lowering the heat; let the spinach cook for 5 minutes, then add the garlic and lemon juice, and stir to combine. Allow the stew to simmer very gently for 10 minutes; serve warm with rice and the quartered lemons on the side.

NOTE: *One option is to add cilantro pesto to this dish for added depth of flavor. Grab a bag from the freezer* (refer to Chapter 2, "Basics"). *I strongly recommend using fresh spinach instead of frozen here.*

Stews and Stuffed Veggies

Cauliflower Stew
(Yakhnet al-Arnabeet)

YIELD: 4 SERVINGS

This dish is a testament to the flair of Lebanese cooks. Everybody agrees that cauliflower is not the most exciting vegetable, yet this stew really does a fine job of showcasing the beleaguered cauliflower. It is scrumptious, light, even addictive! The secret lies in the addition of fresh lemon juice, cilantro pesto, and very little else. Give it a try—I bet you will be glad you did.

Ingredients:

2 cups olive oil

2 large yellow onions, chopped

1 pound beef or lamb stew meat

1 teaspoon salt

½ teaspoon white pepper

½ teaspoon cinnamon

¼ teaspoon nutmeg

3 cups water

½ large cauliflower head (*about 1 pound*), broken up into florets

1 package cilantro pesto (*see Chapter 2, "Basics"*)

½ cup lemon juice

Directions:

1) Heat ¼ cup of the oil in a Dutch oven over medium heat. Sauté the onions until softened. Add the meat and brown. Sprinkle with the salt, pepper, cinnamon, and nutmeg. Pour the water into the pot and bring to a boil. Lower the heat, cover, and simmer gently for 30 minutes.

2) In the meantime, bring a quart of water to a boil. Add the florets and boil for 3 minutes, then drain and discard the water. Dry the florets on clean kitchen towels or paper towels.

3) Heat the remaining oil in a skillet and sauté the florets until golden throughout. Remove the florets from the skillet and drain on paper towels (handle them gingerly to avoid breaking them).

4) Add the florets and the cilantro pesto to the meat broth. Simmer gently for 20 minutes. Pour the lemon juice into the pot the last 5 minutes of cooking. Serve with rice and vermicelli pilaf (*see Chapter 2, "Basics"*).

Stews and Stuffed Veggies

Jew's Mallow Soup (Mulukhieh)

YIELD: 4 SERVINGS

This dish is a glorious one in the eyes of many in Lebanon, Egypt, and the region. The story in Egypt (where this dish originated) is that *mulukhieh* (from the word *muluk*, "kings"), was such a favorite of the *khedive* (sultan) that he would not allow his subjects to eat it (it was purported to be an aphrodisiac). He suffered a sad fate, because one day he went swimming in the Nile and never returned.

The Lebanese, who migrated in droves to Egypt in the nineteenth century, adopted mulukhieh. Upon their return, they introduced it to their fellow countrymen, who created their own versions from north to south. My grandmother used to make it with fresh leaves that she would spread on a white sheet over her queen-size bed and dry for a few hours. She would then stack them up and shred them paper-thin. Today, though, everybody gets it already shredded and frozen at the store to save time and effort. In some communities, the leaf is kept whole, while in others it is minced. In any case, eating it is an event worthy of inviting many relatives and friends.

Ingredients:

1 whole chicken, about 3 pounds

6 cups water

1 bay leaf

1 cinnamon stick

6 whole black peppercorns

½ teaspoon white pepper

salt, to taste

2 cups chopped onions, divided

¼ cup olive oil

2 packages of cilantro pesto (*see Chapter 2, "Basics"*)

1 teaspoon ground coriander

¼ cup lemon juice or white vinegar

1 package frozen chopped *mulukhieh* (14 ounces)

Directions:

1) Place chicken in a Dutch oven with water, bay leaf, cinnamon stick, peppercorns, white pepper, salt and half the onions. Simmer for 45 minutes until tender, skimming any froth from the top.

2) Take out the chicken, cut into serving pieces, and set aside. Strain and reserve broth.

3) In a large pot over medium heat, pour the oil and fry the remaining onions until softened. Add the cilantro pesto, coriander, and strained chicken stock, and bring to a simmer; add the lemon juice then the *mulukhieh*. Heat until the first bubble appears. Serve with the traditional trimmings if desired.

TRIMMINGS: A platter of rice pilaf, a bowl of pita croutons, a bowl of chopped onions soaked in one cup of red vinegar and the chicken pieces.

NOTE: *Salah Hassan, an Egyptian farmer, gave me his mom's secret for* mulukhieh: *she dips a whole tomato in the broth prior to adding the mulukhieh. He swears this method eliminates sliminess. If using the tomato method, don't add lemon or vinegar to the broth.*

Stews and Stuffed Veggies

Potato and Meat Stew
(Yakhnet Batata)

YIELD: 6 SERVINGS

This traditional stew is for a day of cold and wet weather, when one is forced to be tucked away at home. In this stew, cubed potatoes are fried before being added to the stew. You may decide to forego the frying, but I think in this case it adds flavor and richness to the stew.

Ingredients:

2¼ cups oil

2 medium onions, chopped

½ pound stew meat or kafta meatballs (see Chapter 2, "Basics")

½ teaspoon allspice

½ teaspoon cinnamon

½ teaspoon white pepper

3 cups water

1 pound potatoes

1 pound tomatoes (or a 16-ounce can), peeled and diced

¼ cup cilantro pesto, optional (see Chapter 2, "Basics")

Chopped parsley (garnish)

Directions:

1) Heat ¼ cup of the oil in a soup pot over medium heat and sauté the onions. Add the meat and brown for 10 minutes on all sides. Sprinkle the meat and onions with allspice, cinnamon, and pepper. Add the water to the pot, cover, and bring to a simmer. Uncover the pot and skim the froth off the surface. Cover the pot and let the meat and onions simmer for 1 hour over very gentle heat.

2) Heat the remaining oil in a skillet over medium heat. Peel and dice the potatoes and place them in a bowl with water. Drain the potatoes and fry them in the hot oil. Drain. Another option is to drizzle oil, salt, and pepper on the cubed potatoes and roast them in a 375-degree F oven until they take on color.

3) Add the potatoes and tomatoes to the stew. Let the stew simmer for 15 minutes longer. Add the cilantro pesto the last 5 minutes of cooking. Serve with rice pilaf.

NOTE: *Some people make this without adding the tomatoes; in this case, add ¼ cup of lemon juice to the stew at the end. When using kafta meatballs, reduce the simmering time to 20 minutes.*

Stews and Stuffed Veggies

Okra Stew in Tomato Sauce

YIELD: 4 SERVINGS

In Texas, okra is practically a state vegetable, offered fried at every barbecue joint and road stand. Okra *(bamieh)* is also beloved in Lebanon. It is served as a stew or as a side dish (meatless) for a mezze. To make it as a side dish, or to transform it into a vegetarian meal, simply omit the meat from this recipe and serve it at room temperature with pita bread.

Ingredients:

⅓ cup olive oil

2 medium yellow onions, chopped

½ pound stew meat *(to save time, use ground beef)*

1 teaspoon salt

1 teaspoon ground coriander

1 pound okra, frozen *(to use fresh okra, see note below)*

1½ pounds ripe tomatoes, peeled and diced *(or use canned tomatoes)*

¼ cup cilantro pesto, optional *(see Chapter 2, "Basics")*

½ lemon, juiced or 1 tablespoon of pomegranate molasses

Directions:

1) Heat the oil in a Dutch oven over medium heat. Sauté the onions for a few minutes. Add the stew meat (or ground meat) and sprinkle with salt and coriander. Add the okra and panfry for 5 minutes. Add the tomatoes, cover, and stew for 30 minutes until the meat is tender.

2) Add a package of cilantro pesto sauté to the stew the last 5 minutes of cooking, along with the lemon juice.

NOTE: *If you are using fresh okra, cut off the tip of the pod, dry with paper towels, and stir-fry in ½ cup of olive oil; then add to the rest of the ingredients.*

Stews and Stuffed Veggies

Veggie-Stuffed Artichoke Bottoms

YIELD: 4 SERVINGS

Artichokes are wonderful vegetables but they are intimidating—all those leaves, the fuzzy, prickly heart inside—all of this can be discouraging for someone attempting to conquer the artichoke! Artichoke bottoms are available in bags in the frozen section of Middle Eastern markets (imported from Egypt), saving the home cook a lot of time. In Beirut, I met a greengrocer who'd spend time cleaning the artichokes while chatting with his friends. Then he'd sell a batch of bottoms, all cleaned up or prepped for the freezer. This is a special recipe from chef F. Hassan, whose secret touch (adding orange juice and a touch of sugar) makes this dish extraordinary.

Taste of Beirut

Directions:

1) Heat the butter in a skillet over medium heat. Sauté the onions until softened and golden spots appear. Transfer to a bowl. Add the frozen mixed veggies and fava beans to the skillet and stir-fry for 5 minutes. Add to the bowl with the onions and combine.

2) In a deep pot or skillet, boil the water and 1 teaspoon of the salt. Simmer the artichoke bottoms for 7 minutes and transfer to an ovenproof serving dish. Reserve 1 cup of the artichoke water in the skillet.

3) Stuff the artichoke bottoms with the veggie mix.

4) Heat the oven to 325 degrees F. Add the orange juice, lemon juice, garlic paste, remaining salt, pepper, and sugar to the skillet. Add the cornstarch dissolved in water to the sauce and stir until it thickens. Taste and adjust seasoning. Carefully spoon the sauce over the stuffed artichokes. Bake for 20 minutes. Serve garnished with parsley.

Ingredients:

3 tablespoons clarified butter

1½ cups pearl onions, peeled

2 cups cut-up mixed frozen veggies

½ cup fresh fava beans (or frozen or butter beans)

3 cups water

2 teaspoons salt

8 artichoke bottoms

1 large orange, juiced (about ⅔ cup fresh orange juice)

1 medium lemon, juiced (about 3 tablespoons juice)

1 teaspoon garlic paste (see Chapter 2, "Basics")

½ teaspoon white pepper

2 teaspoons sugar

2 tablespoons cornstarch diluted in ⅓ cup water

¼ cup chopped parsley

NOTE: *This dish can be served at room temperature, if desired. Using fresh artichokes will provide the dish with optimal flavor.*

Stuffed Pumpkin
(Titoumi Dolma)

YIELD: 8 SERVINGS

This is a recipe from Mrs. Yvette Tabet, who got it from her friend, Mr. Hourani. *Titoumi* is the Armenian word for pumpkin. However, none of the Armenians I asked in Beirut knew of this dish. It is a showstopping dish, full of sweet-and-sour flavors and reminiscent of Persian cuisine. It would be a nice change for a traditional Thanksgiving table.

Directions:

1) Cut off the top of the pumpkin and set it aside. Remove all the seeds and fibrous flesh inside. Carve the pumpkin so that the shell is thin. Dice the pumpkin flesh and set aside.

2) Cook the rice until it is done but still firm (under-cook it by 3 minutes). Transfer to a bowl and add the diced pumpkin flesh, raisins, barberries (or dried cherries or currants), apple, brown sugar, cinnamon, and salt.

3) Heat the oven to 350 degrees F. Fill the pumpkin with the rice mixture. Pour the water and the butter over the mixture. Place the cap on the pumpkin and wrap the pumpkin in foil. Bake for about 40 minutes or until a knife inserted into the pumpkin comes out easily. Serve by cutting into it, like a cake.

Ingredients:

1 pumpkin
(5 pounds or less)

1½ cups long-grain rice
(American or basmati)

⅓ cup golden raisins

⅓ cup barberries *(or dried cherries or currants)*

1 large apple *(Granny Smith or other green variety)*, chopped

3 tablespoons raw or light brown sugar

½ teaspoon cinnamon

1½ teaspoons salt

½ cup water

½ cup melted clarified butter *(or oil)*

Stews and Stuffed Veggies

Stuffed Tomatoes with Meat
(Banadoora Mehsheyeh)

YIELD: 8 SERVINGS

In this dish, simply pick good, end-of-the-summer tomatoes to stuff, and concentrate on the sauce. The ground meat and onion stuffing can be retrieved from the freezer and the rice pilaf made a half hour before the meal is served *(see Chapter 2, "Basics" for both recipes).*

Ingredients:

8 large tomatoes *(ripe)*

¼ cup olive oil

1 tablespoon garlic paste *(see Chapter 2, "Basics")*

1 can *(28 ounces)* tomato sauce *(plain)*

1 tablespoon pomegranate molasses *(can substitute tamarind paste)*

½ teaspoon salt

½ teaspoon cinnamon

1 teaspoon allspice

1 teaspoon grape molasses *(or honey or raw sugar)*

1 tablespoon paprika or ground Aleppo pepper *(optional)*

1 batch ground meat and onion stuffing *(see Chapter 2, "Basics")*

1 cup fried pine nuts or sliced almonds *(either fresh or from the freezer)*

Directions:

1) Slice the caps off the tomatoes, one inch from the tip, and set aside. Remove most of the flesh from the tomatoes, using a grapefruit spoon if you have one. Transfer the flesh into a bowl, dicing the larger pieces. Sprinkle the tomatoes with salt and flip them over on the counter. Set aside for 20 minutes.

2) Heat the oil in a saucepan over medium heat and sauté the garlic paste for 10 seconds. Add the tomato flesh, tomato sauce, pomegranate molasses, salt, cinnamon, allspice, grape molasses, and paprika. Cover the saucepan. Simmer for 10 minutes over gentle heat. Taste and adjust seasoning.

3) Heat the oven to 325 degrees F. Fill an ovenproof pan with the sauce and place the tomatoes in the pan. Fill each tomato with the ground meat and onion stuffing and cover with the caps. Bake for 20 minutes or so, basting the tomatoes a few times. Serve with a rice and vermicelli pilaf *(see Chapter 2, "Basics")* and garnish with the nuts.

Stuffed Swiss Chard Leaves with Rice and Meat

YIELD: 4 TO 8 SERVINGS

This dish is one of the classics of Lebanese traditional cuisine. It is usually presented with stuffed zucchini as well, however, zucchinis in Lebanon are much smaller and sweeter than the variety found elsewhere, so I decided to only stuff them with the chard, which is comparable. Chard leaves are easier to stuff than grape leaves; the leaves simply get rolled up like a cigar. In addition, they are fresh, which gives a much tastier result than brined grape leaves.

I discovered an even faster technique for stuffing them: instead of cutting the leaves into neat four-inch squares, I thought, *Why not make king-size cigars instead?* I bought two bunches of Swiss chard, and they were beautiful, with huge leaves. I cut the thick stalks *(to use later in a dip; see Swiss Chard Stalks Dip on p. 110)* and rolled up the leaves into extra-long snakes that I curved around to look like a water hose. Simple—and so much easier!

Taste of Beirut

Directions:

1) Bring two quarts of water and 1 teaspoon of the salt to a boil. Drop the chard leaves into the pot for 5 seconds. Remove and drain, then lay flat on your work surface.

2) In a large bowl, mix the ground beef or lamb, rice, 1 teaspoon of the salt, ¾ teaspoon of the cinnamon, ¾ teaspoon of the allspice, and 2 tablespoons of the oil or butter.

3) Sprinkle the remaining salt, cinnamon, and allspice on the lamb chops. Heat the remaining oil in a Dutch oven over medium heat and panfry the lamb chops on both sides. Line the bottom of the pot with the lamb chops.

4) Place a whole leaf flat in front of you and shape about ½ cup of the meat and rice filling into a long and thin sausage and place it on the long side of the leaf. Roll it up like a cigar (not too tight). Do the same with the remaining leaves and rice and meat mixture.

5) Place the rolled chard leaves on top of the lamb chops, coiling them around as necessary until the coils look like a water hose and the lamb chops have been completely covered. Place a small plate on the leaves to hold them in place and gently pour the water into the pot.

6) Bring to a simmer and let the leaves and the rice mixture cook very gently for about 1 hour. Uncover the last 10 minutes of cooking and add the lemon juice to the broth. Taste a couple of grains of the rice to check if it is cooked. Cool the pot for 10 minutes or so, then remove the plate and flip the pot onto a deep serving platter (which will collect the broth). Serve with a bowl of yogurt.

Ingredients:

3 teaspoons salt

2 bunches Swiss chard leaves, washed and cut alongside the stalks (stalks reserved and leaves kept whole or cut into rectangles)

¾ pound ground beef or lamb (or a combination of the two)

½ cup short-grain rice (or sushi rice, Turkish rice, or Egyptian), soaked 30 minutes in water

1½ teaspoons cinnamon

1½ teaspoons allspice

4 tablespoons oil or clarified butter

6 lamb chops (more or less depending on the size of the pot used)

3 cups water

¾ cup lemon juice

1 container (32 ounces) plain yogurt

Stews and Stuffed Veggies

White Beans with Cilantro in Tomato Sauce *(Fasoolia Bel-Zeit)*

YIELD: 8 SERVINGS

This bean stew is vegan. There are dozens of vegan dishes in the Lebanese kitchen. This dish (like most others) can be turned into a stew with meat. This version is served at room temperature with bread. It can be part of a mezze table on a small plate, or it can be served on a platter for a rustic lunch or dinner.

Ingredients:

1 pound white or red beans, soaked overnight

1 tablespoon white or apple cider vinegar

6 cups water

1 teaspoon coriander

½ cup olive oil

3 large onions, chopped

3 pounds Roma tomatoes (*or 3 large cans of tomatoes, diced*)

Salt, to taste

½ teaspoon white pepper

½ teaspoon cinnamon

¼ cup tomato paste

1 package frozen cilantro pesto (*see Chapter 2, "Basics"*), more if needed

Pita bread, to serve

Directions:

1) Soak the beans overnight in 2 quarts of water with 1 tablespoon of white or apple vinegar.

2) The next day, drain the beans and put them in a Dutch oven. Add the water and coriander to the pot. Bring the pot to a simmer and cook the beans for one hour or until tender.

3) Heat the oil in a large skillet over medium heat and sauté the onions until golden. Add the tomatoes, garlic, salt, pepper, and cinnamon.

4) Transfer the tomato mixture to the pot with the beans and add the tomato paste. Simmer for an additional 30 minutes, uncovered. Add the cilantro pesto the last ten minutes of cooking. Taste and adjust seasoning. Serve at room temperature with pita bread on the side.

NOTE: *This stew is also prepared without the addition of the cilantro pesto, to taste; I prefer this version.*

Roasted Turkey with Spicy Rice Stuffing (Habash w-Hashwet al-Ruz)

YIELD: 12 SERVINGS

This is the traditional Christmas turkey served in Lebanon. It is delicious and very fragrant. It would add an authentic Lebanese taste to your American Thanksgiving table.

Directions:

Heat the oil in a Dutch oven over medium heat and sauté the rice until the grains are coated in oil. Add the allspice, cinnamon, pepper, nutmeg, cloves, and salt. Add the ground meat and onion stuffing. Stir the mixture for a few seconds, then add the chicken stock. Cover, lower the heat, and let the mixture cook for 20 minutes. To serve, place the roasted turkey on the platter surrounded with the spiced rice, and garnish with the nuts and chestnuts.

Ingredients:

½ cup oil or clarified butter

3 cups long-grain rice

1 teaspoon allspice

1 teaspoon cinnamon

½ teaspoon black pepper

½ teaspoon ground nutmeg

½ teaspoon ground cloves

Salt, to taste

1 batch ground meat and onion stuffing *(see Chapter 2, "Basics")*

6 cups chicken stock *(more as needed)*

1 preroasted 10-pound self-basting turkey

2 cups assorted roasted nuts *(see "Nuts" in Chapter 2, "Basics")*

2 cups chestnuts in a vacuum-packed bag or can *(optional; see note below)*

NOTE: *If using the chestnuts, empty the contents of the chestnut bag into a strainer and rinse under tap water; pat dry. Melt ¼ cup butter in a skillet and sauté the chestnuts for a minute or so. Add to the other nuts when ready to garnish.*

Rice, Grains, Pasta, and Legumes

Roasted Green Wheat and Lamb Pilaf
(Freekeh Bel-Lahmeh)

YIELD: 4 SERVINGS

In this dish, the lamb shanks can be replaced with chicken legs or thighs. The method is simple: brown the lamb or chicken, season with spices and onions, add water, and simmer until cooked. The resulting broth is used to cook the freekeh, which is served with the meat on a platter.

Directions:

1) Heat ¼ cup of the oil in a Dutch oven over medium heat. Sauté the meat and onions until the meat is browned and the onions have softened. Sprinkle the allspice, pepper, cinnamon, and salt on the meat and onions, cover with the water, and bring to a boil. Lower the heat, cover, and simmer for 1 hour or until the meat is cooked and falls off the bone.

2) Remove the meat from the pot and set aside on a serving platter, discarding any bones or gelatinous bits. Strain the broth into a sieve set over a bowl, pressing on the onion to extract as much pulp as possible.

3) Rinse the freekeh under running water, removing debris. Drain. Heat the remaining oil in the Dutch oven and sauté the freekeh until all the grains are coated in oil. Pour the meat broth over the freekeh (you need to double the volume of liquid to grain) and cover the pot. Bring to a simmer and let it simmer gently for 30 minutes or longer if the grain is still hard. If needed, add a little water and cook it longer. Serve on a platter with meat pieces and fried nuts.

Ingredients:

½ cup oil

1 pound lamb shanks *(or beef stew meat or chicken legs and thighs)*

1 large onion, chopped

1 teaspoon allspice

½ teaspoon black pepper

½ teaspoon cinnamon

Salt, to taste

4 cups water

1 cup freekeh

½ cup fried or toasted mixed nuts *(almonds, pine nuts, and pistachios, or your choice) (see "Nuts" in Chapter 2, "Basics")*

NOTE: *To save time, you may use a batch of ground meat and onion stuffing from the freezer (see Chapter 2, "Basics"). Add it to the freekeh while sautéeing it in butter, pour the water or broth over the freekeh, and cover, cooking for 30 minutes or until the freekeh is soft and chewy. You can make a sauce with any leftover broth. Dissolve 1 heaping tablespoon of cornstarch for each cup of broth in ¼ cup of water. Heat the broth until it steams and add the cornstarch mixture. Stir for a couple of minutes until thickened. Taste, adjust seasoning, and serve.*

Lentil and Bulgur Pilaf
(Mujaddara Hamra)

YIELD: 4 SERVINGS

Taste of Beirut

This lentil pilaf is called Southern Mujad-dara, since it is how folks in the southern areas of the country eat it. The bulgur should be coarse and the lentils should be small and brown. We never ate this type of mujad-dara at home, but now this is my favorite. After cooking, the bulgur turns silky, and its flavor with the lentils is irresistible.

Ingredients:

1 cup brown lentils

3 cups water

4 large onions

1 cup plus 1 tablespoon vegetable oil

1½ teaspoons salt, to taste

¾ cup coarse bulgur (*#3 or #4*)

1 teaspoon cumin

¼ cup flour

Directions:

1) Put the lentils and water in a Dutch oven. Simmer for about 20 minutes.

2) Finely chop 2 of the onions. Heat 3 tablespoons of the oil in a skillet and sauté the onions until golden brown. Add to the lentils.

3) Slice the remaining 2 onions into rings. Sprinkle with 1 teaspoon of the salt and set aside.

4) Add the bulgur to the lentils. Cook the mixture for 20 minutes or so, until the bulgur and lentils are thoroughly cooked and the water has evaporated.

5) About 10 minutes before the end of cooking, add the cumin and the remaining salt. Taste the mixture and adjust seasoning. If the lentils or bulgur are still hard, add half a cup of water and cook a little longer over gentle heat.

6) Heat the remaining oil on medium in the same skillet used to sauté the onions. Put the flour into a large Ziploc bag, add the sliced onion rings, and shake. Fry the onion rings until crispy.

7) Garnish the lentils with the onion rings and serve at room temperature with fresh veggies (definitely radishes!) and a glass of *ayran* (yogurt drink) or a bowl of yogurt and cucumber salad.

Rice, Grains, Pasta, and Legumes

Red Lentil and Rice Pilaf
(Mujaddara Safra)

YIELD: 4 SERVINGS

Nutritionists have found that combining a starch (rice, bulgur) with lentils helps the body absorb the lentils' iron.

In Lebanon, any type of lentil pilaf is called "mujaddara." Thus, the one with green lentils is called "white" mujaddara, with brown lentils, "red" mujaddara, and finally, the one with red lentils is called "yellow." This yellow mujaddara is the easiest to make and tastes just wonderful.

Ingredients:

⅓ cup vegetable oil

2 medium onions, chopped fine

1½ cups red lentils

½ cup short-grain rice *(Italian, Egyptian, sushi, or Turkish)*

6 cups water

Salt, to taste

Directions:

1) Heat the oil in a Dutch oven over medium heat. After 3 minutes, add the onions and sauté until softened and golden. Add the lentils and rice and stir for a few seconds. Add the water to the pot, cover, and bring to a boil. Reduce the heat and simmer for 45 minutes or longer, until the lentil and rice mixture has started to thicken, stirring every once in a while. Add salt to taste. Check the texture of the mujaddara. Once it has thickened, transfer it to a serving plate. Serve warm or at room temperature with a salad, pickles, radishes, and olives if desired.

NOTE: *The rice needs to be short-grain and starchy. For this recipe, using basmati or American long-grain will not work as well. Some people like to add cumin to this dish.*

Rice, Grains, Pasta, and Legumes

Dumplings in Yogurt Sauce
(Sheesh Barak)

YIELD: 40 DUMPLINGS

Making sheesh barak can be compared to making pasta from scratch. The results are superior to anything store-bought, and truthfully, the technique is a lot easier to master than pasta, with only three ingredients required—flour, water, or milk—and a little salt. Busy Lebanese housewives buy the dumplings frozen in the neighborhood market to save time. I prefer to make my own and freeze the extras (they freeze very well). Assembling the dish is easy once the dumplings are ready, because the yogurt sauce and the rice can be prepared at the last minute, and the cilantro pesto can be pulled out of the freezer as well.

Ingredients:

1 cup all-purpose flour

Dash of salt

½ cup milk or water

2 cups kafta
   (see Chapter 2, "Basics")

1 batch cooked yogurt
   sauce *(see Chapter 2,
   "Basics")*

¼ cup cilantro pesto
   (see Chapter 2, "Basics")

1 batch rice pilaf with
   vermicelli
   (see Chapter 2, "Basics")

Directions:

1) Place the flour and salt in a mixing bowl. Add enough water or milk and knead to get a smooth and shiny ball of dough. Transfer to a sheet of plastic and refrigerate.

2) Remove the dough from the fridge and roll it out on a floured counter until very thin (as thin as possible). Cut it into circles (the smaller the better) and fill one half with a teaspoon of the kafta. Fold over and pinch to seal. Pinch both ends to form a shape similar to a tortellini. Place all the dumplings on a greased cookie sheet.

3) Preheat the oven to 325 degrees F. Lightly toast the dumplings, about 10 minutes. (Cool and freeze extras and keep what is needed for this dish at hand.)

4) Pour the yogurt sauce in a medium-size pot over medium heat. Add the dumplings and the cilantro pesto, then simmer for ten minutes. Serve with rice pilaf.

Rice, Grains, Pasta, and Legumes

Lebanese Couscous with Chicken
(Moghrabieh)

YIELD: 8 SERVINGS

This is the Lebanese equivalent of the North African couscous. Its name, moghrabieh, means "a dish from the Maghreb," referring to the North African region comprised of Algeria, Morocco, and Tunisia. This Lebanese version, however, is totally different and specific to Lebanon. Moghrabieh was considered a feasting type of meal and used to be prepared with both lamb shanks and chicken. Nowadays, it is simpler and served with one or the other. In Lebanon, one can purchase the grains (also called moghrabieh) fresh from specialized stores. It is available dried in the United States and other countries.

Moghrabieh keeps well in the fridge for several days and can be reheated in the microwave. It can also be frozen.

Directions:

1) Heat the water, 1 teaspoon of the salt, and 1 tablespoon of the oil in a Dutch oven and bring to a simmer. Boil the moghrabieh grains for 5 minutes, then drain into a sieve set over a large bowl. Set the moghrabieh aside and return the water to the pot.

2) Place the chicken, cinnamon stick, bay leaf, and whole onion in the Dutch oven with the water and bring to a simmer; skim the froth when it appears and discard. When the chicken is cooked, turn off the heat and set it aside to cool a bit. Strain the broth, reserving 2 cups for the sauce.

3) Heat the remaining oil in a large skillet and brown the pearl onions gently; remove the onions and set them aside. In the same skillet, panfry the moghrabieh, sprinkling it with the caraway, cinnamon, allspice, and the remaining salt, adding ladles of the broth, one at a time, until the grains are tender. Add half of the chickpeas and ⅔ of the onions, and simmer for a few minutes.

4) To make the sauce, heat the remaining broth until it steams. Add the cornstarch mixture, the rest of the chickpeas, and the leftover onions. Stir a couple of minutes until thickened; taste and adjust seasoning.

5) Cut the chicken into large pieces, discarding the bones and skin. Serve the moghrabieh by piling it high on a large serving platter, holding it in place with the chicken pieces all around; serve with the warm sauce on the side.

NOTE: *You can buy a moghrabieh spice mix from an Arabic store to save time.*

Ingredients:

6 cups water

2½ teaspoons salt

¾ cup plus 1 tablespoon clarified butter or olive oil

1 pound dry moghrabieh

1 chicken *(about 3 pounds)*

1 cinnamon stick

1 bay leaf

1 large onion, whole

1 pound pearl onions, peeled

1½ tablespoons ground caraway

1 tablespoon ground cinnamon

1 teaspoon allspice

1 can *(15.5 ounces)* chickpeas

¼ cup cornstarch diluted in ½ cup water

Rice, Grains, Pasta, and Legumes

Cabbage and Rice Pilaf (Makmoura) with Cabbage Salad

YIELD: 4 SERVINGS

This dish originally came from Lebanese rural cuisine and was made with bulgur instead of rice. Rice made its entry into Lebanon from the Far East and became extremely popular. A Lebanese saying describes this occurrence: "Rice came and conquered and bulgur hung himself!" *(al ezz lal-ruz w al-burghul shanak haloh)*. The addition of cumin makes the cabbage sparkle. It also helps reduce the bloating commonly associated with cabbage.

Directions:

1) To blanch the cabbage, add about 6 cups of water and 1 teaspoon of salt to a deep pot and bring to a boil. Add half the cabbage for 1½ minutes, then drain it in a colander and rinse it under cold water until it's cool to the touch. Shred the cabbage to get approximately 3 cups.

Ingredients:

3 cups shredded cabbage, blanched and drained

⅓ cup olive oil

1 large onion, chopped

1 teaspoon garlic paste *(see Chapter 2, "Basics")*

1 cup rice *(Italian, medium-grain, sushi, Egyptian)*

2 cups water *(or chicken stock)*

1 teaspoon salt

½ teaspoon white or black pepper

1 teaspoon cumin *(or more, to taste)*

2) Heat the oil in a large saucepan over medium heat. Sauté the onions until golden. Add the garlic and sauté until soft. Add the cabbage, reduce the heat, and stir from time to time for 5 minutes. Add the rice and stir until it is coated in oil and translucent. Add the water or chicken stock, salt, and pepper. Cover and bring the mixture to a boil. Lower the heat and simmer gently for about 20 minutes until the rice is cooked. Take the cover off the saucepan, sprinkle the cumin on top, and serve.

NOTE: *Makmoura is traditionally served with a shredded cabbage salad dressed with lemon, garlic, and olive oil. Some folks in the mountains make this dish with bits of lamb confit (awarma). Choose a medium-size cabbage (in Lebanon they get to a huge size) and cut it in half; use one half for the rice pilaf and the other to make the salad that is served alongside it.*

Falafel Loaf with Tarator Sauce

YIELD: 8 SERVINGS

Falafels have taken America by storm! This chickpea loaf is a falafel minus the deep-frying. It is fluffy and moist. It is eaten with a fork, with some tarator sauce drizzled on top.

Directions:

Heat the oven to 375 degrees F. Drain the chickpeas and transfer them to the bowl of a food processor. Add the eggs, bread crumbs, onion, baking powder, cumin, coriander, paprika, and salt, and process until mixture is doughy. Add the parsley, cilantro, garlic paste, and olive oil, and process until the mixture is smooth and all the ingredients are well combined. Transfer to a loaf pan lined with parchment paper. Bake for 35 minutes or until a knife inserted in the loaf comes out dry. Serve at room temperature with the tarator sauce.

NOTE: *The amount of sauce can vary based on preference. I'd recommend setting aside 1 cup of sauce for the entire loaf, which would give each serving 1 or 2 tablespoons.*

Ingredients:

2 cans *(15.5 ounces)* chickpeas

3 large eggs

½ cup bread crumbs

1 large white onion, chopped

1 teaspoon baking powder

1½ teaspoons cumin

1 teaspoon coriander

1 teaspoon paprika or Aleppo pepper

1 teaspoon salt

1 cup Italian parsley

1 cup cilantro

1 tablespoon garlic paste *(see Chapter 2, "Basics")*

¼ cup olive oil

1 cup tarator sauce *(see Chapter 2, "Basics")*

Rice, Grains, Pasta, and Legumes

Kibbeh Meat Dough
('Ajeenet al-Kibbeh)

YIELD: 1 KIBBEH PIE or 8 SERVINGS

Ingredients:

2 cups extra-fine bulgur
 (#1)

1 onion, quartered

1 teaspoon salt, or to taste

½ teaspoon allspice

½ teaspoon black pepper

½ teaspoon cinnamon

1 pound ground meat,
 extra lean (no trace of fat
 whatsoever; the best cut
 is from the heel of round,
 breast, or flank)

I had planned a little dinner party and wanted to make a dish that would be representative of Lebanese cuisine, yet could be prepared in advance. Kibbeh meat and Kibbeh meat pie are as traditional as it gets; kibbeh was devised as a way to stretch meat, since mixing meat and bulgur would yield double the volume of meat alone. Meat for kibbeh needs to be extra lean.

Directions:

1) Place the bulgur in a bowl and rinse under tap water for a few seconds. Soak the bulgur for about 5 minutes, drain over a sieve, and press on it to extract all the remaining water.

2) Place the onion in the bowl of a food processor and pulse to chop it as fine as possible. Add the bulgur and all the spices and start processing the mixture; add the meat gradually while processing, scraping the bowl once or twice with a spatula. Add ¼ cup of ice water if the dough feels too dry or stiff. The kibbeh dough needs to be moist, firm, and smooth. Transfer to a bowl, cover and keep it in the fridge until needed.

NOTE: *Purists will insist that the best kibbeh is made either using the stone mortar (jeren) or using a meat grinder set at the finest setting. The food processor is currently the most popular and practical option.*

Taste of Beirut

Kibbeh Meat Pie *(Kibbeh Bel-Saniyeh)*

MAKES 8 SERVINGS

Ingredients:

1 batch kibbeh meat dough

1 batch ground meat and onion stuffing *(see p. 32)*

Directions:

1) Make filling *(see Chapter 2, "Basics: Ground Meat and Onion Stuffing")* or retrieve from freezer.

2) Make kibbeh meat dough.

3) Generously grease a 10-inch round pan; roll out one third of the dough on a piece of wax paper (you can cover the top with another piece of wax paper); flip the rolled out dough onto the pan. Cover the bottom with the filling, spreading evenly. Roll out the remaining dough and flip it over onto the filling, lightly patting it down with fingers moistened with ice water. Score the kibbeh (see *"How to Make and Score a Kibbeh Pie"* on the following page); using the handle of a wooden spoon, make an indentation in the middle of the pie.

4) Brush the pie with oil or melted butter, filling the indentation in the middle. Preheat the oven to 350 degrees F and bake the pie for 20 minutes, until the surface is browned and glistening. Serve with Yogurt and Cucumber Salad *(see p. 154)* on the side.

NOTE: *The kibbeh pie can be frozen, cooked or uncooked, for two weeks.*

Kibbeh

How to Make and Score a Kibbeh Pie

1. Roll out dough flip on wax paper, the flip onto pan.

2. Spread filling evenly.

3. Add the top layer of dough in patches.

4. Cover completely, then smooth surface with damp fingers.

5. Start scoring pie, into quarters, then eighths.

6. Score parallel lines within each section.

7. Now score crosswise in each section to form a diamond pattern.

8. Dig hole in the center and score the perimeter. Smother the top with butter.

Kibbeh Meat Balls

YIELD: 40 SMALL BALLS (MORE or LESS, DEPENDING ON SIZE)

Taste of Beirut

Directions:

Prepare the filling first: Transfer the filling to a bowl.

Prepare the kibbeh dough: Fill a small bowl with ice water to which you have added 2 teaspoons of olive oil. This should help in shaping the balls.

How to shape the kibbeh into balls:

1) Put the dough into a bowl and knead it briefly with your hands to get a feel for it and make it as smooth as possible. Shape it into even-sized balls with a cookie dough scooper (1½ inches in size) and set the balls side by side on a piece of foil.

2) Dab your fingers in the ice water, and taking one ball at a time, roll it between your palms until it is even and smooth. Hold the ball in the palm of one hand and form a cavity with the index finger of the other hand. Keep rolling your index finger, as if it was a screwdriver, to form thin "walls"—the thinner the better. Tap gently on the wall of the kibbeh as you turn it around to thin it out, dipping your finger in the ice water as soon as the dough gets sticky. Fill each ball with one or more teaspoons of filling. Dip your fingertips in the bowl of ice water and gently pinch the opened tip to seal it with your thumb and index finger. Pinch on both ends to make the balls look dainty (optional).

3) Heat the oil to 375 degrees F in a deep skillet or pot. Fry the balls for about 3 minutes until browned. Drain and serve.

To save leftover kibbeh balls: Grease a baking dish and place the kibbeh balls in the dish, rolling them gently here and there to coat them in oil. Bake them for 10 minutes on 350 degrees F until browned. Cool the kibbeh and freeze them on a large cookie sheet. Once they are frozen, put them in freezer bags. Take them out of the freezer as needed without defrosting them. They can be dunked in a yogurt or tahini sauce and reheated gently for about 10 minutes.

Ingredients:

Filling:

1 batch ground meat and onion filling *(see Chapter 2, "Basics")*

4 cups vegetable oil

Kibbeh dough:

Use the kibbeh dough recipe *(see p. 234)*

Kibbeh

Kibbeh Saucers
(Kibbeh Sajieh)

YIELD: 30 KIBBEH SAUCERS

This kibbeh is baked rather than fried. It is shaped like a saj, the concave-shaped oven that sits on many street corners in Beirut these days and is used to make flatbreads (man'ooshe). It is filled with fried onions and walnuts, and spiced with hot chili pepper and pomegranate molasses. It is a great kibbeh for a party since you can prepare it in the morning and bake it when your guests arrive. It is usually served with some red pepper dip (muhammara) on the side.

Directions:

1) Prepare the kibbeh dough and set aside. Grease a large baking sheet.

2) Heat the oil in a skillet and sauté the onions until they are golden. Add the walnuts and sauté until slightly toasted and fragrant. Add the hot pepper paste, pomegranate molasses, salt, and pepper, and stir to combine well. Set aside to cool a bit.

Ingredients:

1 batch kibbeh meat dough *(see p. 234)*

Kibbeh filling:

⅓ cup olive oil

2 cups chopped onions

2 cups chopped walnuts

1 tablespoon hot red pepper paste *(or to taste) (may substitute pureed red pepper or pureed canned red bell peppers)*

1 tablespoon pomegranate molasses

1 teaspoon salt, or to taste

½ teaspoon black pepper, or to taste

3) Heat the oven to 375 degrees F. Roll out the kibbeh dough between two sheets of wax paper, as if you are cutting cookies. Cut the dough into round shapes with a 3-inch cookie cutter. Place about 1 tablespoon of the filling on half of the kibbeh circles. Cover with the other circles of kibbeh dough, gently patting around the edges of each circle to seal. Set the filled kibbeh circles on the baking sheet. Bake for 10 to 15 minutes until cooked. Serve with red pepper sauce or red pepper dip (muhammara) *(see recipe on p. 124)* on the side, if desired.

Kibbeh

Kibbeh in a Yogurt Sauce
(Kibbeh Labniyeh)

YIELD: 8 SERVINGS

This was my all-time favorite dish growing up. I loved the creamy yogurt sauce flavored with touches of garlic and cilantro, and the hollow kibbeh balls that I would break open with my spoon in order to dip them in more sauce and stretch the pleasure. *Kibbeh Labniyeh* encapsulates what Lebanese cuisine delivers: a light, healthy, subtly spiced meal.

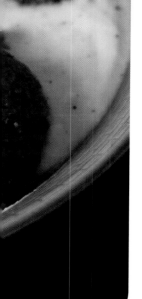

Ingredients:

½ batch kibbeh meat balls *(see recipe on p. 238);* use either frozen *(fried)* kibbeh balls or freshly made kibbeh balls *(not fried)*

1 recipe cooked yogurt sauce *(see Chapter 2, "Basics")*

¼ cup cooked short-grain rice *(Italian, Egyptian, Turkish, or sushi)*

¼ cup cilantro or mint pesto *(see Chapter 2, "Basics")*

Directions:

1) *If using fresh kibbeh balls:* Bring 6 cups of water and a teaspoon of salt to a boil in a large pot on medium-high heat. Puncture the kibbeh balls from both ends with a toothpick prior to poaching them so that they don't burst. Drop the kibbeh balls, a few at a time, into the boiling water and boil for 7 minutes. Drain the balls, reserving the liquid.

2) Gently add the kibbeh balls to the yogurt sauce. When all the kibbeh balls have been added to the sauce, gradually add up to 2 cups of the poaching liquid to the sauce while stirring gently for 10 minutes over low heat. The sauce should start to steam and bubble up. Keep stirring another 15 minutes until the sauce is thick and creamy. Remove from the heat. When ready to serve, gently stir the cilantro or mint pesto into the sauce until it is well incorporated.

If using frozen kibbeh balls: Start heating the yogurt sauce; as soon as it starts to bubble up, drop the frozen kibbeh balls into the sauce and simmer gently until the balls warm up, about 10 minutes. Five minutes before the end of cooking, add the rice and the cilantro pesto. Serve warm.

Kibbeh

Kibbeh Balls in Citrus-Tahini Sauce
(Kibbeh Arnabiyeh)

YIELD: 8 SERVINGS

In Beirut, most of the residents come from elsewhere, usually a town or village in a rural area north, south, or inland, in the Bekaa Valley. Each area has food memories specific to their community. This kibbeh arnabiyeh is a traditional dish claimed by native Beiruti (more precisely, West Beirut, the original and oldest part of Beirut). It is one of the great classics of Lebanese cuisine. Kibbeh balls are poached in a tahini and citrus broth with a spattering of chickpeas and lamb pieces. What makes this dish so special is the Seville oranges, which are only available during a short time (in fact, most Lebanese cooks freeze a good portion of the Seville orange juice to use later in the year). This kibbeh dish is served with rice. Seville oranges are found in Arab or Latino markets and some supermarkets in United States. They are sometimes called "sour oranges." When not in season, Seville oranges can be substituted with a combination of oranges, blood oranges, grapefruits, and lemons in order to achieve that same sweet-and-sour taste.

Ingredients:

1 pound lamb shanks

1 pound extra bones *(optional)*

1½ pounds onions, quartered

1 stick cinnamon

1 bay leaf

6 whole peppercorns

1 teaspoon salt

4 cups water

1 batch citrus-tahini sauce *(see Chapter 2, "Basics")*

⅓ cup cornstarch diluted in ¾ cup citrus juice

25 empty kibbeh balls *(½ batch; see recipe on p. 238)*

1 can *(15.5 ounces)* chickpeas

3 cups cooked rice *(optional)*

Directions:

1) In a pressure cooker or a slow cooker, place the lamb shanks, bones (if using), onions, cinnamon, bay leaf, peppercorns, and salt. Cover with the water and simmer gently for 1 hour or longer, until the meat falls off the bone. Strain the broth, discarding all bones. Set the lamb pieces aside. Boil the stock down to 2 cups.

2) In the same pot, add the citrus-tahini sauce, stirring until steam appears. Add the cornstarch mixture and stir longer until the sauce thickens. Add the kibbeh balls, chickpeas, and lamb pieces. Stir for another 10 minutes or so until the kibbeh is warmed up. Serve with rice.

Kibbeh

Pumpkin Kibbeh Pie
(Kibbeh La'teen)

YIELD: 1 PIE

This kibbeh is commonly prepared in mountain villages during times of fasting. Any type of squash is used, but pumpkin is the most popular. The filling includes dark leafy greens and chickpeas, and is strongly flavored with sumac to add a tangy flavor to the rather mild taste of pumpkin. It is *very* important here to drain the squash thoroughly, in order for the pie to shine with intense pumpkin flavor.

Directions:

1) In a food processor bowl, place the drained bulgur, grated onion and spices; mix a few minutes, then gradually add the dry pumpkin pulp and breadcrumbs. The dough should be moist and firm; add a little of the drained pumpkin water if the dough feels too parched. Store in a covered bowl in the fridge until needed.

2) Heat the oil in a deep skillet over medium heat and fry the onions till golden. Add the greens, chickpeas, and spices, and cover the skillet for a few minutes, until the greens have wilted. Remove from the heat, and taste and adjust seasoning.

3) Preheat the oven to 350 degrees F; generously grease a pie pan and spread with half of the dough. Cover the dough with the filling and the nuts, then top the filling with the remaining dough, smoothing it out with a spatula. Score the pie (see Meat Kibbeh Pie, p. 236) and cover the pie with oil. Bake for 20 minutes and serve warm.

NOTE: *Fresh bread crumbs can be substituted with a few tablespoons of flour or cornstarch (or both). You can garnish the top of the pie with pine nuts before baking, if desired. The greens used for the filling can be briefly boiled in a pot of salted water for a few seconds until limp, then drained and squeezed dry.*

Ingredients:

For the kibbeh dough:

2 cups fine bulgur *(#1) (yellow bulgur preferably)*; use same quantity bulgur as pumpkin flesh

1 medium onion, grated

1 teaspoon ground Aleppo pepper *(or paprika)*

1 teaspoon salt

1 teaspoon coriander

1 teaspoon cinnamon

1 teaspoon allspice

1 teaspoon white pepper

2 cups pumpkin (save pumpkin water) cooked and very well-drained

1 cup fresh bread crumbs

For the filling:

⅓ cup oil

2 large onions, chopped

1 pound Swiss chard, turnip greens or spinach

1 can *(15. 5 ounces)* chickpeas, rinsed and drained

2 tablespoons sumac *(substitute pomegranate molasses if desired)*

1 teaspoon salt

½ teaspoon black pepper

⅓ cup pine nuts *(or almonds or walnuts)*

For the top of the crust:

1 cup vegetable oil or a mixture of olive and vegetable oil

Kibbeh

Pumpkin Kibbeh Balls

YIELD: 8 SERVINGS

Ingredients:

Kibbeh dough:

Use the same dough and seasoning as for the pumpkin kibbeh pie

Kibbeh filling:

Use the same filling as for the pumpkin kibbeh pie

For frying:

4 cups vegetable oil or a mixture of olive and vegetable oil

These vegan kibbeh balls are made with pumpkin and bulgur and stuffed with chard, onions, and walnuts. They were traditionally prepared for fasting days. These vegetarian kibbeh are also called "tricky" or "lying" kibbeh (*kibbeh heeleh* or *kazzabeh*), because they are supposed to look like the meat kibbeh but do not contain any meat.

Directions:

1) For instructions on how to shape the kibbeh balls, refer to the meat kibbeh balls *(see p. 238)*.

2) Stuff with 2 or 3 teaspoons of filling and enclose the kibbeh ball. *(For more detailed instructions, see p. 239.)*

3) Heat the oil and fry the balls for about 3 minutes or until orange-brown and crispy. Serve with some lemon quarters if desired. Tarator sauce is a good sauce to serve these with.

NOTE: *These kibbeh can be boiled in salted, boiling water for a few minutes. Drain and coat in a dressing of garlic paste, lemon juice, and olive oil.*

Kibbeh

Potato Kibbeh Pie
(Kibbeh al-Batata)

YIELD: 1 PIE

Directions:

1) To make the dough, soak the bulgur in water for 5 minutes then drain well, pressing to extract all the water. Transfer the bulgur to the bowl of a food processor. Add the grated onion, salt, allspice, cinnamon, nutmeg, and mint, and process for 30 seconds.

2) Boil the potatoes until well done. Drain and peel. Mash them while they are still hot. Add the potatoes to the food processor with the bulgur and onion mixture, and run the machine for a few minutes, scraping the bowl until the dough is homogenous.

3) To make the filling, heat the oil and sauté the onion slices until caramelized, adding the sugar to speed things up. Add the walnuts, salt, pepper, and pomegranate molasses, and sauté for a couple of minutes. Stir the mixture to combine and set aside.

4) Heat the oven to 350 degrees F. Oil a 10-inch round pan and spread half the kibbeh dough over the pan, patting it with your fingers and palms (dip them in ice water first). Spread the dough with the onion and walnut filling. Spread the remaining kibbeh dough over the filling. With the help of a knife, score the pie into quarters, and each quarter into diamonds. With the back of a spoon, make an indentation at the center of the pie. Cover the entire pie with a generous amount of olive oil, making sure to fill the indentation in the middle *(see images, p. 236)*. Bake for 20 minutes, or until the kibbeh takes on a golden color. Serve hot or at room temperature.

Ingredients:

For the kibbeh dough:

2 cups brown bulgur *(#1 extra-fine)*

1 medium onion, grated

1 teaspoon salt

1 teaspoon allspice

½ cinnamon

½ nutmeg

1 teaspoon dry mint powder

5 medium potatoes

Kibbeh filling:

⅓ cup olive oil

5 medium onions, sliced

1 teaspoon sugar

2 cups coarsely chopped walnuts

1 teaspoon salt

½ teaspoon white pepper

2 or 3 tablespoons pomegranate molasses *(to taste)*

For the top of the crust:

1 cup melted clarified butter or a mixture of olive and vegetable oil

Kibbeh

Fish Kibbeh Pie

YIELD: 1 PIE

Ingredients:

For the kibbeh dough:

1¼ cup fine bulgur #1, soaked 5 minutes and drained very well

1 medium onion, grated

1 teaspoon salt

1 teaspoon black pepper

1 teaspoon ground coriander

¼ teaspoon cinnamon

1 cup chopped fresh cilantro

1 pound white fish fillet, cut into chunks and coated in flour

Rind of one orange

For the kibbeh filling:

½ cup olive oil

5 large onions, sliced

1 teaspoon salt

½ teaspoon white or black pepper

½ teaspoon turmeric or a pinch of saffron

½ cup roasted pine nuts

¾ cup oil to cover the pie before baking

For the top of the kibbeh:

Pinch of saffron or ½ teaspoon turmeric

½ cup olive oil to brush on the surface

We did not grow up eating this type of kibbeh in our household in Beirut. This kibbeh hails from Tripoli, our northern capital and a large seaport. This kibbeh pie is made of one layer of dough spread in a pan with fried onions and nuts underneath. It can be served at room temperature. The same dough can be used to make fish kibbeh balls or domes (recipe follows directly after), or any shape you can imagine. I have also had good luck freezing it, both cooked and uncooked, although I would not recommend keeping it in the freezer for longer than two weeks.

Directions:

1) In the bowl of a food processor, combine the bulgur, onion, and spices, including the cilantro. Add the fish fillet chunks and orange rind and process till the dough is smooth and holds together. Transfer to the fridge and cover till needed.

2) In a large skillet, heat the oil over medium heat. Add the onion and sauté till golden-brown. Add the spices and pine nuts and stir to combine.

3) To assemble the pie, refer to the instructions for the kibbeh meat pie on page 236.

NOTE: *The traditional kibbeh pie with fish is made in one layer only. You spread all of the filling on the bottom and roll out one layer of dough and set it on top of the filling.*

Taste of Beirut

Fish Kibbeh Balls

MAKES 8 SERVINGS

Directions:

Follow the recipe for the Fish Kibbeh Pie, but form balls instead. Place a ball of kibbeh dough on the palm of your hand. Using the index finger of the other hand, dig a hole in the ball and twist your hand repeatedly until the hole gets bigger. Insert 2 teaspoons of stuffing in the hollow kibbeh ball and pinch it closed. Using your fingertips, draw out pointed ends. Set aside and proceed with the other balls until all are done. Place in the fridge until ready to cook.

Kibbeh

Tuna Tagen

YIELD: 4 SERVINGS

A *tagen* in Lebanon is usually a platter with fish and sautéed onions smothered in a tahini sauce. It is a delicious dish but a bit pricey if  the fish is a freshly caught sea bass or grouper. Ever ingenious and resourceful Lebanese housewives came up instead with a tuna tagen, using some humble cans to create the same dish without breaking the wallet. This recipe is from Hoda Sweid, a native Beiruti.Her sister was having a party and served this dish buffet-style. Her guests loved it, totally cleaning up the platter; no one noticed that the fish was canned tuna!

Ingredients:

2 cans *(6 ounces)* tuna in oil

3 large yellow onions, sliced

1½ cups tarator sauce *(see Chapter 2, "Basics")*

1 teaspoon salt, or to taste

½ teaspoon white pepper

¼ cup toasted pine nuts or sliced almonds *(see "Nuts" in Chapter 2, "Basics")*

1 tablespoon cumin *(more as needed)*

Pita bread, as needed, to serve

Directions:

1) Drain the oil from the tuna into a skillet. Heat the oil over medium-low heat and sauté the onion slices for a few minutes until they soften. Cover the skillet for 10 minutes and lower the heat. Uncover the skillet and add the tarator sauce, salt, and pepper.

2) Start adding the tuna to the skillet, breaking it into little pieces with a wooden spoon. Transfer the tagen to a platter and sprinkle it with toasted pine nuts and cumin. Serve with pita bread.

NOTE: *Keep extra cumin on the side for people who like to sprinkle more on their tagen. This tagen sauce can also be served without any tuna as a dip.*

Seafood Dishes

Fish with Rice and Onions
(Seeyadeeyeh)

YIELD: 8 SERVINGS

Seeyadeeyeh (catch of the day) incorporates the best *fresh* fish caught that day, along with glistening browned rice, golden pine nuts, and a caramelized onion sauce. I remember my grandmother announcing triumphantly that she had found a *lokoz* (type of grouper found in the Mediterranean) that met her high standards. This dish is an event. I have found during my stay in Lebanon that it is prepared differently from one coastal city to another. Folks from Sidon like to add other spices to it (saffron, cardamom) and do not caramelize the onions, whereas Beirut natives claim they'd never touch it unless the onions were browned first! This recipe is how we had it, seasoned with cumin and not much else; both versions are exquisite.

In a few words, here is what this dish needs to achieve: the fish head needs to be fried in oil to give flavor to the stock and the onions need to be fried in the fish-flavored oil and caramelized. The fish pieces need to be poached in the fish stock for a few minutes, and the rice needs to cook in the fish stock. You should set aside at least two cups of fish stock to make a cumin-flavored sauce at the end to spoon over the fish and rice. The cumin-flavored sauce is simply the remaining sauce thickened with cornstarch and seasoned with lemon juice and cumin.

Directions:

1) Heat 1 cup of the oil in a Dutch oven over medium heat. Fry the nuts until caramel-colored then remove and set aside. Fry the fish (parts and heads) until browned in the pot. Add the water and salt to the pot and bring to a simmer. Sprinkle with cumin. Cook until done (a few minutes) then remove the fish to a platter to cool. Strain the stock to make sure there are no fish bones in it, and put it back in the pot.

2) Heat the remaining oil in a skillet and fry the onions until caramelized. Transfer them to the Dutch oven with the fish stock. Using an immersion blender, puree the stock with the onions. Reserve 2 cups of the stock to make a sauce later.

3) Bring the remaining stock to a boil, add the rice, and lower the heat. Cook the rice for about 20 minutes, or until done. Taste the rice and adjust seasoning.

4) Separate the large fish pieces, deboning them and discarding the skins.

5) Prepare the sauce by heating the reserved fish stock and the lemon juice. Stir the cornstarch mixture into the sauce when it starts steaming, and it will thicken within minutes.

6) To serve, pile the rice on a platter, place the individual fish portions on top, and the toasted nuts as a garnish throughout. Serve the sauce in a gravy boat on the side, along with some fresh radishes.

NOTE: *The fish head is where the concentrated flavor of the fish is and will really infuse the stock and rice with flavor. I found some fish heads separately packaged at an Asian market, which is a good option if fish heads are hard to find.*

Ingredients:

1½ cups vegetable oil

1 cup pine nuts or sliced almonds

4 pounds white fish (striped bass, grouper, or snapper) cut into 3 parts *(head, body, and tail)*, salted and sprinkled with cumin powder and some flour, if desired

6 cups water

2 teaspoons salt *(or to taste)*

¼ cup cumin

3 pounds yellow onions, chopped

3 cups long-grain rice *(American, jasmine, or basmati)*

2 medium lemons, juiced *(about ⅓ to ½ cup juice)*

¼ cup cornstarch diluted in ⅓ cup water

2 bunches radishes

Spiced Fish, Beirut-Style
(Samkeh Harra Beirutiyeh)

YIELD: 4 SERVINGS

Spiced fish, a glorious buffet-style dish, is one of the culinary masterpieces of Tripoli, Lebanon's northernmost coastal city. Not wanting to be found lacking, Beiruti chefs have come up with their own version. It's easier to prepare and lilting, with the flavor of lemon and the undercurrents of cilantro, garlic, and red chili pepper.

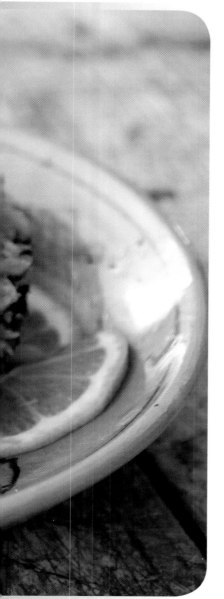

Directions:

1) Season the flour with the cumin and salt. Heat the oil in a large skillet. Dip the fish in the seasoned flour and fry until golden brown. Remove the fish from the skillet and set aside on a platter.

2) Put the cilantro and garlic into the skillet, lower the heat, and fry for a few seconds, until the fragrance lifts up.

3) Flake the fish with a fork, cover with the cilantro and garlic, douse with the fresh lemon juice, and sprinkle with the chili powder. Serve.

Ingredients:

½ cup flour or bread crumbs

2 teaspoons cumin

1½ teaspoons salt

½ cup olive oil

1½ pounds white fish fillets

2 cups chopped cilantro

2 tablespoons garlic paste *(see Chapter 2, "Basics")*

½ cup fresh lemon juice *(more as needed)*

1 teaspoon red chili powder or hot paprika if desired

NOTE: *To save time, use three packets of cilantro pesto from the freezer (see Chapter 2, "Basics") instead of using the fresh cilantro and garlic.*

Seafood Dishes

Calamari with Red Pepper Sauce

YIELD: 4 SERVINGS

Do you eat a plate of deep-fried calamari and feel guilty afterward? I do. This is a tasty and speedy alternative to the fried calamari featured in restaurant menus all over the globe. You can replace the calamari with baby octopus, shrimp, bay scallops, or crab. I used a sauce inspired by our classic red pepper sauce (muhammara).

Directions:

1) Cook the pasta according to the package directions. Drain and pour 1 tablespoon of the oil on it. Toss a bit, cover, and set aside in a 170-degree F oven.

2) Dry the calamari slices on paper towels. Heat the remaining oil and fry the onion for 7 minutes or until golden. Add the red pepper paste, water or clam juice, cumin, garlic paste, pomegranate molasses, walnuts, anchovy paste, ketchup, pepper, and chili pepper sauce (if using). Cook for 5 minutes, stirring from time to time to mix the ingredients well.

3) Add the calamari and stir for 15 seconds over medium heat; cover. Uncover the pan and check the calamari. If the rings look opaque (after about 5 minutes), they are done. Toss the calamari sauce and the pasta together well. Serve piping hot with quartered lemons.

Ingredients:

8 ounces of angel hair pasta

⅓ cup plus 1 tablespoon of olive oil

1 pound calamari (*fresh or frozen*), sliced in rings in the package

½ batch red pepper sauce (*see p. 124*)

1 tablespoon anchovy paste

1 tablespoon ketchup

¼ teaspoon black pepper

Dash of chili pepper sauce (*optional*)

2 lemons, quartered (*or limes*)

Seafood Dishes

Shrimp in a Pineapple Boat

YIELD: 8 SERVINGS

A dish that spells summer, and definitely a beach party!

Taste of Beirut

Directions:

1) Place the shrimps in a saucepan, add the water (or clam juice) and simmer for 5 minutes or until they turn pink. Remove, cool, then peel the shrimps and set aside. Reserve the stock.

2) In a saucepan, over medium heat, pour ¼ cup of oil; add the moghrabieh, salt, white pepper, and paprika, and stir 4 minutes. Add the shrimp stock, cover and simmer for 30 minutes or until the grains are chewy, adding ½ cup more water if needed.

3) In a skillet, over medium heat, pour ¼ cup of oil and sauté the pineapple chunks, diced red pepper, jalapeño, cashews, and shrimps briefly; add the sugar, pineapple juice, remaining oil and spices and stir a bit to combine. Add the moghrabieh and toss. Line the pineapple halves with lettuce and fill with the salad; garnish with the chopped herbs when serving.

Ingredients:

1 pound large shrimps

2 ½ cups water
(or clam juice)

¾ cup oil, divided

1 cup moghrabieh
(or small elbow pasta)

Salt, to taste

1 teaspoon white pepper

2 teaspoons paprika

1 large pineapple, cut in half and cored, chunks set aside

1 cup diced red bell pepper

¼ cup diced jalapeño pepper

1 cup cashews

1 tablespoon brown sugar or honey

½ cup pineapple juice

½ teaspoon turmeric

1 teaspoon chili powder

Lettuce leaves (iceberg or butter lettuce)

½ cup chopped cilantro, parsley, or dill

Seafood Dishes

Breaded Scallops with Mango Sauce

YIELD: 4 SERVINGS

Ingredients:

1 pound sea scallops

Marinade Ingredients:

1½ teaspoons salt

1 tablespoon grated orange
rind *(or any citrus)*

1 teaspoon garlic paste
(see Chapter 2, "Basics")

2 teaspoons grated
fresh ginger

½ teaspoon hot ground
Aleppo pepper or paprika

⅓ teaspoon white pepper

2 cups kataifi dough,
chopped

¾ cup flour

2 small eggs

2 large fresh and ripe
mangoes, peeled and
diced

½ cup water

2 teaspoons lemon juice

2 teaspoons white sugar

2 tablespoons chopped
cilantro

2 cups oil

What could be better on a warm summer evening than to savor some scallops in a kataifi shell against a delicate and fruity mango sauce? Kataifi is the dough commonly associated with Middle Eastern pastries such as *kunafa*.

The delicate sea scallops, coated with the extra-crisp kataifi, is savored in bite-size pieces. The tangy and smooth mango sauce sparkles with hints of cilantro and saffron. Any other seafood or fish fingers can be substituted here.

Directions:

1) Place the scallops in a bowl, along with the marinade ingredients. Stir gently to combine, cover, and let marinade for one hour in the refrigerator.

2) Chop the kataifi dough by pulsing in a food processor till reduced to ¼-inch sticks. Transfer to a bowl. Place the flour in a bowl and place the eggs, lightly beaten, in another bowl.

3) Purée the mangoes in a blender with the lemon juice, sugar, cilantro, and water.

4) Heat the oil to 375 degrees F. Drain the scallops, dip into the flour bowl, egg bowl, and, finally, kataifi bowl. Fry until golden and serve with the mango sauce.

CHAPTER 7

Desserts

Arabic-style pastries in Lebanon are
usually bought from specialized pastry shops.
These shops are well known, and their experience of
decades, if not centuries, is highly respected.
Most home cooks would not dream of emulating
a pastry shop. On the other hand, there are simple
desserts such as puddings and cookies that the home
cook takes pride in offering to family and especially
visitors. There is a well-known Lebanese proverb:
"Your appetite is a reflection of your love
for me (my cooking)" *(Al-akl ala ad-almahabbeh)*.
In essence, if the visitor does not honor the
hostess by eating her food, it implies he
is not well-meaning toward her.

My grandmother, like many others, would make a weekly supply of milk pudding, or *muhallabieh*. She'd make ma'amoul for Easter and anise-ring cookies. Baklavas (*bakleweh*) were store-bought and only consumed on special occasions.

Arabic pastries can be divided into two main categories: the ones made with kadaifi dough (*osmalliyeh*) and the ones made with phyllo (*kellage*). Each category includes dozens of varieties with names such as king's crowns *(taj al-muluk)* or sparrow's nests *(esh al-bulbul)*, and filled with either a thick cream or roasted nuts. The dough is usually fresh and pastries are dunked in syrup, and displayed on huge copper trays in multitiered levels.

This chapter combines both home-style and old-fashioned Arabic desserts, since most people do not have the benefit of an Arab pastry shop nearby! All the pastries in this chapter are easy to prepare.

The simple puddings, such as milk or clementine cream, are always thickened with cornstarch or wheat starch and can be prepared at the spur of the moment. These desserts are offered at the end of a lavish meal but also with coffee during a social visit. The traditional rice or wheat berry puddings are usually prepared once a week in a supply adequate for consuming daily and for offering to drop-by visitors.

The two main flavorings in Lebanese desserts, pastries, jams, confections, and sweet breads are rose water and orange blossom water. Rose water is the distilled water of rose petals gathered during the blooming season of a certain type of rose called *al-ward al-joory* or *Rosa damascena*. Orange blossom water is distilled from the blossoms of a variety of oranges called *boosfeyr* or Seville oranges.

It is also used in folk medicine. My grandmother would give me some orange blossom water in a small Turkish coffee cup at night when

I complained about a tummy ache in order to soothe me and put me to sleep.

Most traditional desserts, in rural areas especially, were sweetened with molasses, specifically, carob or grape molasses; each region would produce the molasses locally and use it in lieu of sugar, which was not yet available or very expensive. (For more details, see Chapter 1, "The Lebanese Larder".)

Quick and Easy Baklava

YIELD: 2 DOZEN PIECES (or ENOUGH FOR ONE 9 X 14–INCH TRAY)

I was watching a TV food show in Beirut about an Arabic pastry shop. I saw the pastry chefs in the back dunk the pastries in hot melted ghee. It would fry to a beautiful golden brown in seconds, then they would take it out swiftly, drain it, and submerge it again, this time in syrup.

I realized a commercial establishment does not have the time to gingerly coat every strand of kunafa or phyllo dough in melted butter. This is what I am suggesting for this one tray of baklava. With this technique, you will spend much less time and effort making your pastries. The extra butter gets thoroughly drained, while leaving that crisp, rich-tasting golden layer of dough scented in rose and orange blossom fragrance.

Taste of Beirut

Directions:

1) Mix ⅓ cup of the syrup with the nuts and set aside. Preheat the oven to 375 degrees F. Grease the bottom and sides of a rectangular pan approximately the same size as the phyllo sheets.

2) Remove one half of the phyllo sheets from the package (keep the other sheets covered with a damp towel until ready to use). Place the phyllo sheets flat in the pan and cover evenly with the syrup-coated nuts. Place the other half of the phyllo sheets over the nuts. Run a spatula all around the pan until the phyllo is neatly tucked in. With a sharp knife, cut the baklava into 3 columns and 4 rows, and then cut the squares diagonally, resulting in 24 triangles. Mix the butter and oil and pour it over the top.

3) Bake the baklava for about 30 minutes or until golden brown. Remove the pan from the oven and carefully drain the excess butter into a bowl by holding the pan at an angle. Pour the remaining syrup over the baklava and let it soak for a few hours uncovered. Serve garnished with the pistachio powdered nuts, if desired. To store, keep in a box tightly closed for 2 weeks.

Ingredients:

2 cups syrup (see Chapter 2, "Basics")

3 cups coarsely chopped nuts (I used peeled pistachios)

1 package (16 ounces) phyllo dough, defrosted according to package directions

3 cups clarified butter, melted (see Chapter 2, "Basics")

½ cup vegetable oil, melted ghee, or samneh (sold at Middle Eastern markets)

1 cup powdered pistachio nuts or other garnish (optional)

Desserts

Carob Molasses and Tahini
(Dibs Be Theeneh)

YIELD: ONE SERVING

Ingredients:

1 teaspoon carob molasses
(or grape molasses)
(more, to taste)

2 tablespoons tahini

Pita bread or crackers

My Teta Nabiha and my aunt Claire would pull out the *dibs* and tahini from the cupboard to eat with a piece of bread or cracker (kaak) late at night when a desire for something sweet was voiced. A proverb from South Lebanon says: "He can lick the *dibs* from the tahini," meaning, "He is so skilled, nothing is too difficult for him."

Directions:

Put some carob molasses and tahini on your plate; stir to mix the two as you desire. Take a piece of pita bread, a cracker, or breadstick, and dip it in or slather some on the bread with a spoon.

NOTE: *Use only carob, grape, or date molasses. It is not recommended with pomegranate molasses, which is used only for savory dishes. Some folks like to dip lettuce or cucumber sticks in this sweet dip.*

Rice Pudding (Ruz B-Haleeb)

YIELD: SERVES 4 to 6 PEOPLE

Taste of Beirut

½ cup short-grain rice
*(I used sushi, but Egyptian
or Turkish rice works
well also)*

2 cups milk

1 vanilla bean *(optional)*

½ cup sugar

1 teaspoon rose water

1 teaspoon orange blossom
water

Directions:

1) In a saucepan, put the rice and add enough water to cover the rice by one inch, bring to a boil, and simmer for about 20 minutes.

2) Add the milk and bring the mixture to a boil.

3) Split the vanilla bean and scrape the seeds into the pot, stirring to distribute them evenly throughout.

4) Lower the heat and let the mixture steam and simmer gently. Stir as often as possible to prevent the milk from burning and scorching the bottom of the saucepan.

5) Add the sugar and keep stirring.

6) When the rice mixture is thick and creamy, add the rose water, and orange blossom water, stirring a few more seconds.

7) Pour the rice into individual serving cups and serve at room temperature or chilled.

NOTE: *This pudding is also made with wheat berries. The method is the same, however the wheat berries need to be soaked in water overnight, and take longer to cook.*

Pomegranate and Milk Pudding

YIELD: 8 SERVINGS

I concocted this dessert one day when I noticed that the pomegranates sitting on the counter were getting very ripe. I recommend making it with fresh pomegranate juice, not bottled juice. To juice the pomegranates, I put the arils in a food processor and run the machine for 20 seconds, and then transfer them into a strainer, pressing on the processed pomegranates to retrieve as much juice as possible.

Make a muhallabieh with milk, sugar, cornstarch, and rose water (or vanilla if you like). Then make the pomegranate cream the same way. Layer the muhallabieh and the pomegranate pudding a tablespoon at a time, switching from one to the other, into ramekins or crystal glasses. You will get nice red and white layers—and a very pleasant tangy-creamy taste. Garnish with the leftover arils.

Ingredients:

Muhallabieh with milk:

2 cups whole milk (*substitute ½ cup whipping cream for ½ cup of the milk for a creamier texture*)

¼ cup sugar

3 tablespoons cornstarch

1 teaspoon rose water or vanilla

Pomegranate cream:

2 cups fresh pomegranate juice

¼ cup sugar or more (*to taste*)

3 tablespoons cornstarch

1 teaspoon rose water or rose syrup

½ cup pomegranate arils, for garnish

Directions:

1) To make the muhallabieh, heat 1½ cups of the milk and the sugar in a saucepan over medium heat, stirring until the sugar is dissolved. Dissolve the cornstarch in the remaining ½ cup milk. When the milk starts to steam, add the cornstarch mixture and stir. When the mixture thickens, add the rose water or vanilla and stir well. Set aside.

2) To make the pomegranate cream, heat 1½ cups of the pomegranate juice and the sugar in a saucepan over medium heat, stirring until the sugar is dissolved and the mixture starts steaming. Dissolve the cornstarch in the remaining juice and add to the pan. Stir until thickened. Add the rose water and stir to combine.

3) One tablespoon at a time, pour the muhallabieh and pomegranate cream into individual ramekins or bowls. Garnish with pomegranate arils. Cool in the refrigerator uncovered. Serve cold.

Red Velvet Pudding (Muhallabieh)

YIELD: 8 SERVINGS

It is not often that both my son and daughter *agree* on things. However, they concurred in saying that red velvet cake was their *all-time favorite cake*. Both also made it clear that they would love to eat it, if I cared to make it. Okay, guys; I understand. I am just not ready, nor willing, to devote a few hours to making a tiered cake with frosting that will contain—at the minimum—6 cups or almost 2 pounds of sugar (in the recipes I found for it, at least). Instead, I compromised: How about muhallabieh, the Lebanese custard (that does not contain eggs or lots of sugar), with a red velvet flavor?

To make the crust:

1) Grease an 8-inch springform pan. Put the chocolate wafer crumbs and melted butter in a bowl and mix to combine. Transfer to the pan and press on the crust with the back of a spoon to adhere it well to the bottom. Put the pan in the freezer.

2) Pour the milk and whipping cream into a saucepan over medium heat. Add the sugar, cornstarch, cocoa, vanilla, and red food color and stir continuously (about 10 minutes) until thickened. Pour the red velvet cream over the crust, cool, and refrigerate.

Ingredients:

Crust:

1½ cups chocolate wafer crumbs (*I used Oreos minus the filling*)

4 tablespoons unsalted butter, melted

Red velvet cream:

2 cups whole milk

2 cups whipping cream (*or half-and-half or milk*)

1 cup white sugar

¾ cup cornstarch

⅓ cup unsweetened cocoa powder

1½ teaspoons vanilla extract

1 tablespoon red food color

NOTE: *I have made this cake with store-bought chocolate cookie crumbs to save time. Use 1½ cups of chocolate cookie crumbs and 4 tablespoons of melted butter, mix, press into the cake pan, bake for 5 minutes in a 325-degree F oven, and store in the fridge.*

Molasses Cake *(Sfoof w-Debess)*

YIELD: 16 SERVINGS

More than a hundred years ago, our fore-fathers in Lebanon and throughout the region used to sweeten their food with molasses. There are many types of molasses made locally; some are produced commercially and exported, and can be purchased at Arab and Mediterranean groceries in North America or online. The best molasses, however, is made either at home or by artisans and farmers in mountain villages.I tasted homemade grape molasses *(dibs el-enab)* at the home of Milady, one of my mom's friends. This 85-year-old lady had made it herself with a sweet variety of grapes. It was sweet and creamy with a color and taste that reminded me of toffee.

This cake is reminiscent of gingerbread. It takes just minutes to prepare and makes a satisfying snack. It used to be sold in Beirut on street carts; now one can find this cake in all Arabic pastry shops in the city. It is often glazed with syrup to keep it moist longer.

Ingredients:

2 cups fine semolina

1¼ cups white all-purpose flour

1 tablespoon ground anise *(omit if you don't like the taste and replace with ½ teaspoon cinnamon)*

1 teaspoon baking powder

¾ cup oil or melted, unsalted butter

1 cup milk *(or water)*

1 cup grape molasses *(or date, carob, apple, or fig molasses, or honey)*

¼ cup tahini to grease the pan *(or you can use cooking spray)*

½ cup pine nuts *(or almonds)*, soaked in 1 cup of water for 1 hour, drained and air-dried

Directions:

1) Pour the semolina, flour, anise powder, and baking powder in a food processor or mixer and mix well. Add the oil or butter and pulse until it is the texture of bread crumbs. Add the milk and then the molasses until the batter is smooth.

2) Heat the oven to 350 degrees F. Smear a baking dish (10-inch round or a 9 × 13–inch pan) with tahini. Pour the dough into the dish, spreading it with a firm spatula. Decorate the cake batter with pine nuts or almonds and score the cake if desired. Bake for about 30 to 40 minutes, until the cake is dry. Cool and serve.

NOTE: *You may like your cake extra-moist; one option is to douse it with a cup of syrup when pulling it out of the oven. Refer to the Chapter 2, "Basics," for the syrup recipe, but make half the quantity of syrup.*

Desserts

Oatmeal Cookies

YIELD: 25 TWO-INCH COOKIES

These oatmeal cookies are similar to cowboy cookies. They are chock-full of "good for you" ingredients, with the addition of halvah, if you have a jar lying around. Grape molasses can be substituted with honey (or date syrup). Both are available at Middle Eastern stores or online.

Directions:

1) Melt the butter and halvah in a saucepan (or a microwavable bowl) over medium heat, stirring every few seconds until the mixture turns creamy and smooth. Transfer to the bowl of a mixer and add the sugar, molasses, and egg. Mix for several minutes at medium speed until the mixture is creamy.

2) Meanwhile, mix the flour with the baking soda, baking powder, nutmeg or cardamom, and cinnamon. Add to the batter and mix. Add the oats, raisins, cranberries, walnuts, and coconut. Mix gently to combine.

3) Preheat the oven to 350 degrees F. Using a tablespoon or cookie dough scoop, form small mounds of cookie dough and place them on a baking sheet lined with parchment paper.

Ingredients:

4 ounces *(1 stick)* unsalted butter, cut into chunks

½ cup halvah *(or replace with tahini and ¼ cup more sugar)*, crumbled

½ cup raw sugar

¼ cup grape molasses *(or honey or date molasses)*

1 large egg

1 cup all-purpose flour

½ teaspoon baking soda

1 teaspoon baking powder

¼ teaspoon nutmeg or cardamom

½ teaspoon cinnamon

3 cups oats

⅓ cup raisins

⅓ cup dried cranberries

⅓ cup toasted walnuts *(or pecans)*

½ cup sweetened, grated coconut *(up to ¾ cup)*

4) Bake the cookies for about 12 minutes or until puffed up and light golden. Immediately remove from the heat and cool on a wire rack. Serve.

NOTE: *The raw cookie mounds can be frozen as is and stored in the freezer for up to two weeks. When needed, remove a few frozen cookies, bake (for a few minutes longer), and enjoy. You can substitute your choice of dried fruit or nuts in this recipe.*

Spice Pudding (Meghli)

YIELD: 8 TO 10 SERVINGS

This is a traditional pudding. It is made on the occasion of a new birth and is passed around to visitors, relatives, and friends. It contains no eggs or cream and is thickened with rice flour. It is spiced with caraway, anise, and cinnamon (in some communities ginger and cardamom as well). These spices were reputed to give strength to the new mother. The name of this pudding, *meghli*, means "boiled." This pudding is very easy to make but requires time simmering over the stove. A lot of home cooks in Lebanon prefer to make it in a pressure cooker. It is also available everywhere (including in North America) in a box as a mix. In addition, meghli spice mixes can be found at Middle Eastern stores.

Today, meghli is available year-round in Lebanon. It can be found at delis, supermarkets, coffee shops, and juice bars in the refrigerated section next to rice puddings, Jellos, and muhallabieh (milk puddings). It is also served for Christmas in some homes and restaurants to celebrate the birth of Christ.

This recipe calls for rice flour, which is available in Arab stores and mainstream supermarkets. If you are unable to find a source for rice flour, one option is to grind rice in a coffee grinder until powdery.

Ingredients:

1 cup rice flour

8 cups water

2 cups granulated sugar

1 tablespoon ground caraway

1 tablespoon cinnamon

1½ teaspoon ground anise *(more to taste)*

Garnishes: Grated coconut, pine nuts, walnuts, pistachios, almonds *(the nuts need to be soaked in water for one hour and drained before using)*

Directions:

1) Soak the flour in 4 cups of the water for 2 hours (or longer) before making the pudding. This allows the rice particles to swell up a bit, thus reducing lumps when cooking.

2) Add the sugar, caraway, cinnamon, and anise to the remaining water in a heavy-bottomed saucepan over medium heat and bring to a simmer.

3) Pour the flour and water over the spiced water. Bring to a boil over medium heat. Reduce the heat and stir to dissolve. Stir every couple of minutes, until the pudding thickens, about 45 minutes to one hour.

4) Transfer to a large platter or individual serving bowls. Garnish with the grated coconut and top with scattered nuts. Store in the fridge and serve cold. The pudding can be stored for a week in the fridge.

Clementine and Milk Cream
(Balouza, Modern-Style)

YIELD: 8 SERVINGS

This dessert is easy to prepare and looks impressive. It is inspired by a traditional milk and fresh orange juice pudding called *balouza*, which consists of milk pudding (muhallabieh) topped with fresh orange cream and served in individual ramekins.

Puddings are thickened with starch (cornstarch or wheat starch) and do not use eggs. The rule of thumb is: Use 1½ tablespoons of cornstarch for every cup of liquid. Use more, say, 2 tablespoons per cup, if you like the pudding to be thicker. Add sugar to taste, a drop of flavoring (orange blossom water and rose water), and you are done. I have added a bit of *amardeen* syrup to the clementine juice for a deeper flavor, but this is an optional step.

Amardeen is an apricot paste from Syria that is exported all over the world, primarily to Middle Eastern markets. It is sweet and tangy, with an intense apricot flavor. It used to be an after-school snack for kids in Lebanon before the invasion of chips. Amardeen syrup is also available in bottles (especially during the holy month of Ramadan when nourishing drinks are so crucial). If you'd like to add that enticing apricot flavor, then going with a bottled syrup is definitely easier. (The paste needs to be soaked in water overnight, heated up a bit, then mixed with water in a blender.)

This dessert is easy to prepare and looks good! The only slight difficulty lies in scooping out the clementine pulp delicately so as not to tear the shell. An easier option is to serve it in pretty glass cups, the traditional way (milk cream at the bottom). The deep orange color is a result of adding *amardeen* (apricot) syrup to the clementine juice. Amardeen syrup is found in all Middle Eastern groceries or online. Its intense apricot flavor pairs very well with the milk cream and deepens the taste of the clementine juice.

Ingredients:

1 cup clementine juice
  (about 12 clementines)

½ cup amardeen syrup or 1 large piece of amardeen sheet, chopped up and soaked in ¾ cup of hot water overnight and pureed in a blender

¾ cup white sugar

¼ cup plus 3 tablespoons cornstarch

2 teaspoons orange blossom water

1 cup whole milk

1 cup whipping cream
  (or whole milk)

Directions:

1) Put the clementine juice, amardeen syrup, and enough water to measure 2 cups in a saucepan over medium heat. Add ½ cup of the sugar and ¼ cup of the cornstarch and stir until the mixture thickens, adding 1 teaspoon of the orange blossom water at the end. Spoon into glass cups or the hollowed-out clementines.

2) Place the milk, cream, remaining sugar, and remaining cornstarch in a saucepan. Stir over medium heat until thickened, adding the remaining orange blossom water at the end. Spoon gently over the clementine cream. Cool, cover, and refrigerate.

NOTE: *The amount of sugar can be altered without affecting the texture of the cream. The orange blossom water is a traditional flavoring (or rose water), but could be substituted with others, such as vanilla.*

Halvah and Chocolate Bars

YIELD: 8 SERVINGS

Halvah is the Lebanese (and Middle Eastern) equivalent of peanut butter. I was told by a former Lebanese army general that halvah is a daily breakfast item for those enlisted. I was also told that it is a breakfast item for inmates. Halvah is an easy and nutritious sandwich for kids in school, and there are many children in Lebanon who are fed a halvah roll-up with Lebanese pita bread. Halvah is made with tahini and syrup, and is slathered on sesame basket bread (kaak) plain or with sliced bananas. I devised this simple dessert for those of us out there who are halvah devotees.

Directions:

1) Grease the bottom of an 8-inch brownie pan. To prepare the crust, place the cookies and sugar in the bowl of a food processor and process, adding the melted butter gradually. Stop when the cookies are reduced to a powder. Pat the crust over the bottom of the pan, using a sheet of plastic wrap over the cookie crumbs to apply pressure with your fingers. Place the pan in the freezer while you prepare the halvah cream.

2) Pour 1 cup of the whipping cream into a saucepan. Add the halvah. Place the pan over medium-low heat and stir gently until the halvah has dissolved. Remove from the heat.

3) Sprinkle the gelatin over the water in a microwavable bowl and heat in the microwave for 10 seconds to melt the gelatin. Pour into the saucepan, stirring for a few seconds.

4) Remove the pan from the freezer and pour the halvah cream into it. Refrigerate for a few hours until firm.

5) To make the chocolate ganache, pour the remaining whipping cream into a saucepan and place over medium heat. Chop the chocolate in a food processor and add it to the saucepan when the cream has tiny bubbles on the surface. Add the honey and stir until the chocolate has melted completely. Pour the chocolate cream over the halvah tart once the halvah cream is cold and firm.

Ingredients:

8 ounces plain cookies *(can use graham crackers or cheesecake crumbs) (1½ cups)*

2 tablespoons sugar

3 tablespoons melted, unsalted butter

1⅔ cup whipping cream

8 ounces halvah, broken into chunks

2 teaspoons plain gelatin *(powder)*

2 tablespoons water

1 bar *(4½ ounces)* dark or semisweet chocolate

1½ tablespoons honey *(optional)*

Yogurt Cheese Mousse with Berries

YIELD: 4 SERVINGS

I had been seeing so many mousses made with mascarpone or cream cheese. I thought, *Why not labneh?* Labneh, or yogurt cheese, does have a bit of sourness from the yogurt, but when it is made into a mousse, the sourness disappears. Enjoy a light and airy mousse made with yogurt cheese, either store-bought or homemade, with a medley of berries and a surprise shortbread cookie resting at the bottom of the glass on top of the berry sauce.

Ingredients:

2 large eggs

⅓ cup powdered sugar

1 cup yogurt cheese *(see Chapter 2, "Basics")*

½ teaspoon vanilla extract

1 teaspoon orange blossom water

1 cup fresh or frozen raspberries

2 tablespoons dark cherry jam *(or any berry jam)*

1 tablespoon granulated sugar *(or more, to taste)*

1 teaspoon lemon juice

4 shortbread cookies

1 cup fresh assorted berries

Directions:

1) Separate the yolks from the whites of the eggs. Beat the whites into a meringue until stiff and glossy.

2) Place the yolks and powdered sugar in a mixer bowl and beat until light-colored and very stiff. Add the yogurt cheese and vanilla. Fold gently until combined and transfer the mixture to the bowl with the meringue.

3) Using a whisk or a spatula, fold the mix into the meringue in an up-and-down motion (so as not to deflate the beaten eggs) until the meringue is no longer visible. Cover with plastic and keep refrigerated until serving time.

4) Place the raspberries, cherry jam, sugar, and lemon juice in a blender and mix until pureed. You can strain the puree if you like. Transfer to a bowl and set aside.

5) To assemble the mousse, pour 2 tablespoons of the raspberry sauce into 4 cups. Place a cookie on top, add a few dollops of the mousse, and top with an assortment of fresh berries. Serve immediately.

Anise Rings *(Kaak Bel-Yansoon)*

MAKES 40 RINGS

These rings are fragrant with anise and very crunchy. They are easy to make as well, and they keep for a while in a tin box. I make them with extra-virgin olive oil from our olive trees in Deir el-Qamar, Chouf.

Ingredients:

2 cups all-purpose flour

¾ cup sugar

Dash of salt

1½ teaspoons baking powder

1 teaspoon ground anise powder

½ cup olive oil

1 teaspoon whole anise seeds

1 egg, plus 1 egg white beaten slightly with a fork

2 tablespoons lemon juice, more or less as needed

1 cup toasted sesame seeds *(optional)*

Directions:

1) Heat the oven to 350 degrees F. Sift the flour, sugar, salt, baking powder, and ground anise into a bowl. Add the oil, anise seeds, and whole egg, and mix. Add the lemon juice, 1 tablespoon at a time, until the mixture holds together and is still moist.

2) Form ½-inch or thinner 6-inch-long sticks. Pinch the ends to form a ring. Dip in the egg white, then dip in the sesame seeds. Place on a parchment-covered baking sheet and bake for 10 minutes or until golden. Cool and serve.

NOTE: *These anise rings are not traditionally dipped in sesame seeds; this is an extra step that I like to follow out of love for sesame seeds.*

Cream
(Home-Style *Ashta* Method)

YIELD: 2½ CUPS

European pastries use elaborate creams based on custards. Arabic pastries only use pure cream, called *ashta*. Pure cream, however, is not easily prepared at home. In Lebanon, anyone needing cream can very easily pick up a container of ashta at a pastry shop. For those who still wish to prepare their own, a simplified ersatz version of ashta was devised, called home-style ashta, or *ashta baytiyeh*. The homemade version is adequate and very simple to prepare. Another option is to use whole-milk ricotta cheese, drained for a few hours and whirled in a food processor until creamy (or not; the clotted cream has a thick texture). The ricotta can be sweetened and flavored with orange blossom water and will keep its thick and creamy texture. The very best ashta I have tasted was sold in Iraq, and it came from buffalo milk.

Directions:

The day before:

Remove the crust from the bread and cut the bread in squares or whirl it in a food processor into bread crumbs. Place the bread in a saucepan with the milk and cream. Cover the saucepan and soak overnight in the fridge.

The next day:

Dissolve the cornstarch in the water. Remove the bread crumb mixture from the refrigerator and place it over medium heat. Stir from time to time, add the sugar, and when the mixture starts steaming, add the cornstarch water. Stir continuously for 2 minutes, until the cream thickens. Add the rose water and orange blossom water and remove from the heat. Cool and store in the fridge covered for a few hours. If you find that your cream is not thickening sufficiently, quickly dilute 1 tablespoon of cornstarch in ¼ cup water and add it to the steaming saucepan while stirring continuously. It should thicken within 1 minute.

Ingredients:

3 pieces American-style white bread *(like Wonder bread)*, soaked overnight in the fridge

1 cup whole milk

1 cup whipping cream

1 tablespoon cornstarch dissolved in ¼ cup water *(more if needed)*

1 tablespoon sugar *(if you are serving the dessert with a syrup, omit the sugar)*

1 teaspoon rose water

1 teaspoon orange blossom water

NOTE: *All Lebanese creams and puddings are thickened with cornstarch (or wheat starch). Sometimes you will find that the cornstarch is not sufficient and the cream or pudding is not getting thick. In these cases, it is okay to add more cornstarch, starting with ½ a tablespoon diluted in 2 tablespoons of liquid to get it thicker within minutes.*

Pistachio Paste

YIELD: 2½ CUPS

Ingredients:

2 cups toasted and peeled
   pistachios *(see "Nuts" in
   Chapter 2, "Basics")*

½ cup almond flour

½ cup syrup
   (see Chapter 2, "Basics")

¼ cup vegetable oil
   (such as canola)

Directions:

1) Place the pistachios in a bowl. Pour boiling water over the nuts and let them cool. Rub with your fingers and the peel will come off easily. Drain and spread the pistachios on a clean towel to air-dry.

2) When the pistachios are dry, toast them 10 minutes or so in a 325-degree F oven or in a skillet on the stove. Cool them and then transfer them to the bowl of a food processor and run the machine for a few minutes. Heat the syrup in a saucepan over low heat. With the food processor running, add the almond flour through the feed tube. Add the hot syrup, and then the oil. You may need to add a bit more oil, depending on the texture. If the dough holds together well and is moist, then it is done.

NOTE: *This paste is rather dense. To make a paste suitable for ma'amoul cookies, combine the pistachios with a syrup that has not been cooked as long, say 7 minutes of simmering time. On the other hand, this paste will do fine incorporated into cake dough, like brownies or cookies.*

Pistachio Ice Cream
(Booza al-Fustuk)

YIELD: 4 SERVINGS

Ingredients:

¼ cup pistachio paste

2 cups vanilla ice cream

Arabic ice cream is the most delicious ice cream, and its history in Lebanon goes back a long time. There is a story about King Solomon enjoying ice cream made from snow shipped from the Lebanese mountains. Traditional Lebanese ice cream includes many fruits, such as mulberries, apricots, lemons, and strawberries, or flavors such as rose, pistachio, or milk. Unfortunately, it includes an ingredient, sahlab, that is not available in the West. It can be found in Lebanon at spice shops or in Turkey (I bought some at the bazaar in Istanbul). Sahlab comes from a variety of wild orchids. It has a most remarkable effect on ice cream, as it makes it chewy. Sahlab is also used to make a drink with milk and sugar. The drink itself is also called sahlab, and boxes of sahlab mix are sold in all Arab groceries in North America.

The following recipe is very easy and does not call for a hard-to-find ingredient. The effort required to make pistachio paste will pay off, as you will be able to use it in many ways (and store it for a long time in the fridge). You can double or triple the recipe, if needed.

Directions:

Place the vanilla ice cream and the pistachio paste in the bowl of a food processor. Mix until the mixture is homogeneous and the pistachio paste has been totally incorporated. Transfer to a bowl and cover with plastic wrap; freeze until solidified. Serve.

Konafa Cake with Nuts
(Osmalliyeh)

YIELD: 8 TO 10 SERVINGS

This recipe from my Egyptian friend Phoebe Hanna is beloved throughout the Middle East, and we once made it together for a girls' night out. The type of pastry used in this dessert can either be baked or fried. Most commercial pastry shops fry it for expediency and crispiness. It is called *osmalliyeh* in Lebanon and is available fresh at specialized pastry shops. This cake will keep well for about a week and can be reheated in individual portions in the microwave for a few seconds.

Taste of Beirut

Directions:

1) Preheat the oven to 375 degrees F. Place the dough in a large bowl. Spread apart the strands of dough with your fingers and pour the butter and oil mixture over them little by little, making sure to cover all the strands. Divide the dough in half. Spread each half in a 9-inch cake pan. Gently press on the dough to fit it snugly into the pan.

2) Bake until the cake is golden and crispy all over, about 20 minutes. Drain the excess butter from the cake pans by slanting them sideways. Flip one half of the cake onto a serving platter. Cover it with the toasted nuts, then place the other half of the cake on top. Pour the syrup over the cake and let it soak in for a couple of hours or longer at room temperature. Serve.

Ingredients:

1 box *(16 ounces)* shredded phyllo dough

3 cups *(total)* clarified butter mixed with ½ cup vegetable oil *(see Chapter 2, "Basics")*

2 cups syrup *(see Chapter 2, "Basics")*

3 cups nuts, coarsely chopped and toasted *(your choice)*

NOTE: *The traditional and popular osmalliyeh in Lebanon is filled with clotted cream (ashta; see recipe on p. 292). In order to save time, you can fill it with whole-milk ricotta that has been previously drained in a sieve for a few hours to remove any extra whey. If desired, the cheese can be sweetened or unsweetened and the syrup served separately. You can also fill it with nontraditional chocolate mousse or a fruit-based cream of your choice. If you fill the cake with cheese, cream, or mousse, plan on serving it that day or within twelve hours. If using ashta, the recipe in Chapter 2, "Basics," will give you only two cups or so. I would increase it by a half to yield three cups of ashta.*

Sweet Fritters (Uwaymate)

YIELD: 45 FRITTERS

Taste of Beirut

These fritters were always prepared by our *teta* (grandmother) for Epiphany, piled high, glistening with syrup. She made them as small

as marbles. I have not seen anyone else make them as small and dainty as hers since. Today these are found in every pastry shop in Beirut, albeit in a larger size. To get them extra crispy, it is recommended that they be double-fried, then dipped in sugar syrup. However, even if they're only fried once at the last minute, they will taste delicious and will be fun to eat as a onetime treat.

Ingredients:

1 cup all-purpose flour

1 teaspoon baking powder

Dash of salt

1 medium baking potato, boiled in water and peeled

1 teaspoon oil

1 egg

½ cup water *(or more)*

2 cups syrup
 (see Chapter 2, "Basics")

6 cups oil, for frying

Directions:

1) Mix the flour, baking powder, and salt in a bowl. In another bowl, mix the potato, oil, and egg. Mix the flour and potato together and add enough water to make a dough. Cover the dough and set it aside for 30 minutes.

2) Shape the fritters as small or as large as you like. As you shape them, place each one on a greased, foil-lined baking sheet.

3) Heat the oil to 375 degrees F and fry the fritters until golden, flipping them gently all around. Remove with a slotted spatula and drain. Immediately soak them in the sugar syrup. Serve.

NOTE: *If you like to double-fry, the first time, fry them half the time, drain them, and then fry them again right before serving. Drain them and soak them in the sugar syrup before serving.*

Ma'amoul Bars with Cream
(Ma'amoul Madd Bel-Ashta)

YIELD: 9x13-INCH PAN (16 PIECES)

Ma'amoul are *the* holiday cookies across the board. They are made for every religious celebration and sold in all Arabic pastry shops with a selection of fillings (pistachio, walnut, almonds, cheese, or date paste). My grandmother used to make them for Easter, infusing the dough with incense. She would painstakingly crimp each cookie by hand with brass tweezers, or use wooden molds (available in Middle Eastern shops), with shapes indicative of the various fillings and connoting religious symbols. Ma'amoul bars are made just like the cookies, but are faster and easier to produce. The semolina dough is made in minutes the day before to give it time to soak up the butter.

Directions:

The night before:

Combine the semolinas, sugar, and mahlab in a bowl. Add the butter, mix well, cover, and set aside overnight.

The next day:

Add the baking powder, rose water, and orange blossom water, and knead the mixture until the dough is smooth and flexible, adding more water if it is too stiff. Let it rest covered for 30 minutes.

To make the cream filling:

Put the milk, cream, sugar, and cornstarch in a saucepan over medium heat. Stirring constantly, bring the mixture to a simmer and stir until thickened. Add the rose water and orange water and mix well. Add the ricotta and mix until fully incorporated. Set aside.

To make the ma'amoul bars:

1) Preheat the oven to 375 degrees F. Grease a 9 × 13–inch pan. Press half of the semolina dough over the bottom of the pan as evenly as possible. Sprinkle with the ground pistachios. Pour the cream filling over the top and spread it evenly with a long spatula.

2) Roll out the other half of dough on a piece of baking paper, then place it on top of the cream filling, spreading it out as evenly as possible. Place the pan in the fridge for 1 hour to firm it up, then score the surface into squares.

Ingredients:

3 cups semolina *(coarse or fine, or a combination of the two)*

½ cup powdered sugar

½ teaspoon mahlab *(optional)*

1 cup melted clarified butter *(see Chapter 2, "Basics")* or oil

1 teaspoon baking powder

¼ cup rose water *(more if needed)*

¼ cup orange blossom water *(more if needed)*

1½ cups ground pistachios *(or other nuts)*

2 cups syrup *(see Chapter 2, "Basics")*

Cream filling:

1½ cups whole milk

1½ cups whipping cream *(or half-and-half or milk)*

¼ cup sugar

7 tablespoons cornstarch

1 tablespoon rose water

1 tablespoon orange blossom water

1 cup whole-milk ricotta cheese, drained overnight over a sieve

3) Bake the ma'amoul bars for 30 minutes or until they turn a deep golden brown. Douse them with syrup (or serve the syrup on the side), cool, and refrigerate.

Dried Figs Preserve
(Mrabbah al-Teen)

YIELD: 3 CUPS

Ingredients:

1½ cups sugar

1½ cups water

½ tablespoon fresh lemon
  juice, strained

½ tablespoon ground anise

1 cup walnuts, soaked in
  water one hour, drained,
  and chopped in large
  pieces

1 pound dried figs, cut up
  in large pieces

¾ cup sesame seeds,
  toasted in a skillet over
  gentle heat

3 mastic pebbles, crushed
  in a mortar with a dash of
  sugar until powdery

Figs are dried at the end of summer in Lebanon. This preserve is made with dried figs, a handful of walnuts, and a smidgeon of toasted sesame seeds. It is spiced with anise and mastic, which imparts a beguiling and exotic flavor. This fig preserve is offered as a dessert or a snack (in rural areas especially) or in traditional homes.

The preserve is easy to prepare and is a perfect snack. It makes a thoughtful hostess gift.

Directions:

1) Place the sugar and water in a heavy-bottomed pan. As soon as the syrup boils, add the lemon juice and stir for a second. Remove froth from the top and discard it.

2) Add the anise, walnuts, and figs. Simmer the mixture gently for about 15 minutes or so, stirring frequently so as not to let it stick to the bottom of the pot.

3) When the syrup has almost evaporated, add the sesame seeds. Stir for a few minutes until the mixture is very thick. Turn off the heat, add the ground mastic, and stir vigorously to mix it well. Let the mixture cool. Pour into a sterilized jar and close tightly. It will keep for up to one year. After opening the jar, store in the fridge.

Taste of Beirut

Glossary

Akkawi: A firm white cheese used in a number of sweet and savory dishes; this cheese is desalted when used in desserts.

Amardeen: An intensely flavored, sweet and tangy apricot leather. It is eaten as a snack, or made into puddings or juices especially during Ramadan.

Areesheh: A traditional cheese resembling ricotta, it is served as a dessert with honey or as a stuffing for turnovers or hand-pies.

Awarma: A lamb confit that is made traditionally in rural areas after slaughtering a sheep. A portion of the meat is cooked in its own fat and preserved for the entire year. It is used to flavor food, as a stuffing, or as a topping with eggs for flatbreads.

Basterma: A cured meat covered with a spice paste. It was introduced into Lebanon by Armenians who took refuge in the country around the time of WWI.

Bulgur: Parboiled wheat grains that are ground in coarse to extra fine grades. Bulgur is used to make kibbeh, as a pilaf, or in tabbouleh. It was a staple food in Lebanon in rural areas.

Carob molasses: A syrup extracted from carob pods. In Lebanon, carob molasses was traditionally used as an alternative to sugar. Mixed with tahini, it is still eaten as a dessert or a snack.

Citric acid: It is sold in Middle Eastern stores and looks like a white powder. It is used to give a lemony taste to foods and to set the color of vegetables.

Clarified butter or ghee: Ghee was a favored fat traditionally, but has been recently abandoned in favor of vegetable oils. Clarified butter can easily be made at home (*see* Basics) and imparts a delicious flavor.

Date molasses: A thick syrup extracted from dates and used in many sweet recipes.

Freekeh: Roasted immature wheat berries, with a powerful, smoky, nutty taste. Freekeh contains up to four times the fiber content of brown rice and is rich in calcium, potassium, iron, and zinc.

Ghazl al-Banat: Similar to cotton candy, this sweet is available in all Arabic pastry shops and sold overseas in some Middle Eastern markets.

Grape molasses: A syrup extracted from sweet white grapes. It was used in rural areas as a sweetener for drinks, puddings, or pastries.

Halloumi: A hard white cheese manufactured in Lebanon but originally from Cyprus. It is made from either cow's or sheep's milk. It is popular grilled or pan-fried in butter.

Hawthorn berries (*za'aroor*): These are berries from the hawthorn tree; they are made into an infusion, believed to be good for the heart, or a traditional jam.

Jellab: A traditional drink, especially popular during Ramadan, and made of grape molasses, raisins, sugar, and rose water. The drink is flavored with incense and garnished with pine nuts and raisins.

Jreesh: Similar to bulgur, this whole grain consists of wheat berries cracked coarsely. It is popular in southern Lebanon and is incorporated in flatbreads, pilafs, and kibbeh mixtures.

Kammouneh: A blend of spices used in southern Lebanese cuisine. It is made of dried and fresh spices. It is combined with meat for frakeh, or boiled vegetables and bulgur to make vegetarian kibbeh.

Kashkawan: This is a firm yellow cheese from sheep's milk, with a salty, slightly pungent flavor resembling parmesan, although not brittle and with a rather moist texture. It is used in sandwiches, grated in pasta dishes, or as topping for flatbreads or turnovers.

Kema: A variety of wild mushrooms or truffles, these are usually foraged by Bedouin tribes in the Syrian Desert and believed to appear after a storm. They are sold fresh in Lebanon and canned overseas. They are used in stews, fritters, and omelets.

Keshek: A white powder with a flavor reminiscent of buttermilk, this is a traditional food in the rural areas and is made from bulgur and milk (and, or, yogurt), then fermented, dried, and ground. It is incorporated into soups, as a topping for flatbreads, or as a stuffing for turnovers.

Kibbeh: A traditional and versatile dish combining lean meat, fish or boiled vegetables with bulgur. Kibbeh comes in dozens of shapes and flavors and is one of Lebanon's national dishes.

Labneh: This cheese is obtained by draining yogurt until it is completely dry. It is then salted and served in a ramequin with a drizzle of olive oil.

Lentils: Lentils are a staple food and come in three varieties: green, brown, and orange. Each is prepared a bit differently, but always in a vegetarian dish with a starch such as rice or bulgur.

Mahlab: A spice used primarily in baking, it comes in seeds or powder and is reminiscent of bitter almond in taste. It is extracted from cherry pits.

Majdoulah: This is a white cheese, similar to mozzarella, presented braided. It is a good melting cheese and is also available with nigella seeds.

Malban: A Levantine version of nougat or divinity candy, this sweet is stuffed with chopped pistachios and offered with tea or coffee.

Mastic: A resin extracted from a small evergreen tree found in Greece and other Mediterranean countries. It is used to add a distinctive taste to puddings, jams, ice cream, and meat marinades (*meskeh*).

Moghrabiyeh: A coarse-grained couscous made from semolina. It is available fresh in Lebanon and dry outside of the country. It is cooked in pilafs and combined with chicken or lamb shanks.

Mulukhiyeh: A famous and traditional dish from Egypt that has been adopted in Lebanon. It is a soup made from the leaves of an herb called jew's mallow; it can be easily cultivated in warm and dry climates and is rich in iron. It is available frozen or dried in Middle Eastern shops and can be found fresh in Asian supermarkets.

Myrtle berries (*hemblass*): These berries are picked from a native bush and eaten raw as a snack or made into a liqueur and candied.

Orange blossom water (*mazaher*): A fragrant water distilled from the blossoms of Seville oranges, used in pastries, desserts and puddings.

Osfoor: Considered a poor man's saffron (its aspect is similar, but the taste inferior to real saffron), this spice is used in pilafs or stews.

Pomegranate molasses: A fruit syrup extracted from a sour variety of pomegranates. It is used as a condiment in many savory stews, stuffed vegetable dishes, meat pies, and side dishes.

Rose water (*mawared*): Distilled from the petals of the Damascus rose, it is used in desserts, sherbets, and syrups.

Sheep tail (*leeyyeh*): A traditional fat from the fat-tailed sheep, it is sold in all butcher shops in Lebanon. It adds flavor to stews or eggs, or as a stuffing. It is one of the main ingredients of lamb confit.

Seven-spice mix: Typically, a combination of nutmeg, ginger, allspice, fenugreek, cloves, cinnamon and black pepper. Seven-spice mix is used in recipes in which minced meat is a primary component.

Semolina: Ground from wheat, semolina comes in fine (*ferkha*) or coarse (*smeed*) grades and is used in making pastries (ma'amoul), puddings, or breads.

Seville oranges (*busfeyr*): A variety of oranges with a distinctive sour taste. Orange blossom water is extracted from their blossoms, and their juice is used in lieu of lemon in many traditional dishes. Their peel is candied and served to guests with coffee or tea.

Sujuk: A spicy sausage popular throughout the Levant, it is fried with eggs, or on its own, or grilled in a shawarma-type of sandwich. It can also be prepared with ground meat and spices without being shaped into casings.

Sahlab: A whitish powder obtained from a variety of dried orchids. It is used in the preparation of a hot drink (of the same name) and to make ice cream.

Sumac: A wild bush with reddish clusters of berries harvested, dried, and ground into a powder. Sumac is used as a substitute for lemon, or as a main component in the Lebanese *zaatar* mix.

Soapwort root (*shelsh al-halawa*): These are the dried roots of the soapwort plant. The roots are boiled into a froth and combined with a sugar syrup to obtain a meringue-like cream. The cream is called *natef* and is served with pastries.

Tahini (*t-heeneh*): A paste made from ground and hulled sesame seeds. It is used in Lebanese cuisine like mayonnaise, combined with vegetables or legumes for dips, as a dressing in sandwiches, and as a sauce in soups and stews. Tahini is a source of the healthy fatty acids omega-3 and omega-6, and is rich in calcium.

Tamarind (*tamarheendi*): The pods of the tamarind tree are boiled into a thick paste and made into a juice, which is especially popular during Ramadan; otherwise, tamarind paste is sometimes used to add a sour taste to a dish instead of lemon.

Tarator: This is the name given to tahini dressing and is made up of tahini, water, lemon juice, and garlic. It is used to dress boiled vegetables, falafel, and other sandwiches like shawarma, and a multitude of dips such as the famous hummus.

Verjuice: A juice extracted from sour grapes, which is used traditionally in lieu of lemon juice such in stuffed vegetables dishes, or as a salad dressing.

Zaatar: A wild (or cultivated) herb, similar to oregano. It is dried and ground into a mix of the same name (with sumac and sesame seeds), and used primarily as a topping for flatbread for a traditional breakfast.

Index

chicken
  chicken bites with dukkah, 128–129
  chicken wings, 182–183
  grilled chicken sandwich (*sheesh
    tawook*), 86–87
  Lebanese couscous with chicken
    (*moghrabieh*), 228–229
  walnut and chicken stew (*Circassian
    chicken sharkasieh*), 196–197
chickpea and potato ball (*topig*), 120–121
chickpea and yogurt casserole (*fattet
  al-hummus*), 70–71
chickpeas with cumin (*balila*), 190–191
cilantro, 4
  cilantro pesto (*aliyyet al-kuzbara*), 25
cinnamon, 5
citrus
  citrus-tahini sauce (*arnabiyeh*), 27
  taro in citrus-tahini sauce, 72–73
clementine and milk cream (*balouza*),
  284–285
couscous (*moghrabieh*), 9–10
  Lebanese couscous with chicken
    (*moghrabieh*), 228–229
cream, homestyle dessert, 292–293

D

dandelion greens salad (*salatet al-hindbeh*),
  150–151
dukkah spice mix, 130–131
dumplings in yogurt sauce (*sheesh barak*),
  226–227

E

eggplant and peppers salad (*al-raheb*),
  164–165
eggplant cake (*Yvette's maghmoor*), 180–181
eggplant dip (*baba ghanouj*), 122–123
eggs, 6
  eggs poached in tomato stew (*beyd
    bel-banadoora*), 60–61
  eggs with potato (*mfarket el-batata*),
    62–63
  omelet with parsley and onion (*ejjeh*),
    64–65

F

falafel loaf with tarator sauce, 232–233
falafel sandwich, 94–95
fattoush salad, 148–149
fava bean soup (*ful mudammas*), 66–67
figs, dried preserve (*mrabbah al-teen*), 302
fish, 3
  fish kibbeh balls, 253
  fish kibbeh pie, 252
  fish with rice and onions (*seeyadeeyeh*),
    256–257
  grilled fish with walnut sauce, 176–177
  po'boy sandwich, 92–93
  spiced fish, Beirut-style (*samkeh harra
    beirutiyeh*), 258–259
  tuna tagen, 254–255
flatbread with keshek (*man'ooshet keshek*),
  82
fritters, sweet (*uwaymate*), 298–299

G

garlic, 4
  cilantro pesto (*aliyyet al-kuzbara*), 25
  cream (*toom*), 31
  paste, 30
grains
  bulgur pilaf, 23
  lentil and bulgur pilaf (*mujaddara
    hamra*), 222–223
  lentil soup with Swiss chard (*adass bel-
    hamud*), 98–99
  red lentil and pumpkin dip, 112–113
  red lentil and rice pilaf (*muaddara
    safra*), 224–225
  rice pudding (*ruz b-haleeb*), 272–273
  roasted green wheat and lamb pilaf
    (*freekah bel-lahmeh*), 220–221
  traditional lentil soup (*adass soup*), 102
grape molasses (*dibs el enab*), 14
green beans and tomato stew (*loobieh
  bel-zeit*), 156–157

H

halvah (*halawa*), 14
  halvah and chocolate bars, 286–287
herbs, 4
hummus, 5

classic hummus (*hummus m'tabbal*),
114–115
hummus with meat (*hummus bel-
theeneh bel-laham*), 116–117
red pepper hummus, 118–119

J

Jew's mallow soup (*mulukhiek*), 202–203

K

kafta pie with tarator sauce, 172–173
kafta sandwich, 88–89
kammuneh, 18–19
kataifi (also *kadaifi* and *osmalliyeh*), 14–15
kebabs (*see* beef, kafta)
kibbeh
    fish kibbeh balls, 253
    fish kibbeh pie, 252
    kibbeh balls in citrus-tahini sauce
      (*kibbeh arnabiyeh*), 244–245
    kibbeh in yogurt sauce (*kibbeh labniyeh*),
      242–243
    kibbeh meat balls, 238–239
    kibbeh meat dough (*ajeenet al-kibbeh*),
      234
    kibbeh meat pie (*kibbeh bel-saniyeh*),
      235–237
    kibbeh saucers (*kibbeh sajieh*), 240–241
    mock kibbeh tartare (*muhammara*),
      170–171
    potato kibbeh pie (*kibbeh al-batata*),
      250–251
    pumpkin kibbeh balls, 248–249
    pumpkin kibbeh pie (*kibbeh la'teen*),
      246–247
konafa cake with nuts (*osmalliyeh*), 296–297

L

lamb, 6
    grilled lamb chops, 178–179
    hummus with meat (*hummus bel-
      theeneh bel-laham*), 116–117
    kafta pie with tarator sauce, 172–173
    lamb in yogurt sauce (*laban ummo*),
      192–193
    mini meat pies (*sfeeha*), 138–139
    roasted green wheat and lamb pilaf

(*freekah bel-lahmeh*), 220–221
lamb confit (*awarma*), 15
Lebanon, 1
legumes, 6
lemons, 3–4
lentils (*see* grains)

M

ma'amoul bars with cream (*ma'amoul madd
    bel-ashta*), 300–301
mahlab (*mahlab*), 16
mastic (*meskeh*), 16–17
mezze, 104–105
mint pesto (*aliiyet al-na'na'*), 34–35
molasses cake (*sfoof w-debess*), 278–279

N

nutmeg, 5
nuts, 6
    pistachio ice cream, 295
    pistachio paste, 294
    toasted and roasted, 36
    walnut sauce, 52–53

O

oatmeal cookies, 280–281
okra stew in tomato sauce, 206–207
olive oil, 4–5
olives, 5
    olives in spiced tomato sauce (*salatet
      zaytoon*), 132–133
okra stew in tomato sauce, 206–207
onions, 4
    tahini and onion sauce (*tagen*), 46–47
orange blossom water, 17
orchid powder (*sahlab*), 18

P

parsley, 4
pasta
    pasta with red lentil sauce, 186–187
    pasta with yogurt sauce, 184–185
pepper, black, 5
pepper, white, 5
phyllo dough, 18